Painful Tears *of*

JOY

Living Proof of God's Faithfulness and Miracles

Weeping May Endure For a Night,
But Joy Comes In the Morning

Debra Lynn Viteri

WESTBOW
PRESS®
A DIVISION OF THOMAS NELSON
& ZONDERVAN

WestBow Press books may be ordered through booksellers or by contacting:

WestBow Press
A Division of Thomas Nelson & Zondervan
1663 Liberty Drive
Bloomington, IN 47403
www.westbowpress.com
1 (866) 928-1240

ISBN: 978-1-5127-3048-7 (sc)
ISBN: 978-1-5127-3049-4 (hc)
ISBN: 978-1-5127-3047-0 (e)

Library of Congress Control Number: 2016902249

Print information available on the last page.

WestBow Press rev. date: 07/08/2016

Contents

Dedication

This book is dedicated, first and above all, to the glory of God and His faithfulness, *"And, we know that in all things God works for the good of those who love Him, who have been called according to His purpose"* (Romans 8:28).

To Joe: You are my husband, best friend, lifelong companion, and partner. You have always encouraged, challenged and supported me, to live my life the best I can for God, our family, and others. I am so grateful for everything you have taught me. You have always stood by my side and allowed me to be challenged to be obedient to the call of God on my life.

When God put us together, it was for more reasons than one. I am honored I was chosen to save your life; this world would be incomplete without you. I am so excited and anticipate the future together serving our Lord. I love you with all my heart. *"And, now these three remain faith, hope, and love. But, the greatest of these is love"* (1 Corinthians 13:13).

To Bethany: You have learned the key in life, to always press on and to never give up! Perseverance is what I see in you; you have persevered under trial and have come out refined. You have matured into a beautiful, fun, loving woman who wants to honor Jesus. Continue to stay strong; God has great and mighty plans in store for you. You are so special, and I'm so proud to call you my daughter. *"Blessed is the man who perseveres under trial, because when he has stood the test, he will receive the crown of life that God promised to those who love him"* *(James 1:12).*

To Jessica: Your fun loving, care free spirit, brought joy in times of difficulty. You were a breath of sunshine, always going out of your way to make us feel loved. You are flourishing into a beautiful woman, who has an obedient, tender heart for God. Obedience is what I see in you. Always be courageous for the Lord, He will take you places you can never imagine. You are so special and I'm so proud to call you my daughter. *"The Lord Himself goes before you and will be with you. He will never leave you nor forsake you. Do not fear nor be afraid; do not be discouraged"* *(Deuteronomy 31:8).*

To My Parents: You both have given of your love unconditionally, and have instilled important values in my life as a child, which makes me the woman I am today. Thank you for all your love, support and prayers for me and my family. I love you both so very much. *"Children's children are a crown to the aged, and parents are the pride of their children"* *(Proverbs 17:6).*

Acknowledgments

I want to acknowledge my in-laws, Edwardo and Teresa and all of Joe's siblings Eddie, Frank, Maria, Rosa, Carlos, Diego, and Jim who were always by our side while we spent many days and weeks in the hospital. Thank you for all your prayers, love and support. We love you so much.

I also acknowledge my sister-in-law, Rosa. Thank you for opening your home and giving us all your love, care and support. You went the extra mile to help restore Joe's life. Thank you for always welcoming our family with open arms and for that, we will forever be grateful. We love you dearly.

I want to acknowledge all of our extended family and friends who had such a tremendous part of the miracle in our lives. Thank you, for listening to the Lord as He woke you up at all hours of the night to pray. You all played an important role in the healing and restoration of our family. Knowing, we had such tremendous support in prayer was a comfort and assurance to continue to walk by faith despite its grim appearance.

Thank you for showing your love to us with delicious meals, baked goods, flowers, cards, visits and gifts of money. We could never have completed this tremendous task without your support and love.

I also want to acknowledge all the liver specialists at New York-Presbyterian Hospital. The team, from the ER, the staff at the liver center, nurses, doctors, and surgeons who without your professionalism, empathy, care and wisdom would have never turned out with such a positive outcome. As well as the post-transplant patients Vito, Rich, and donor Maryann who were kind enough to give me much needed and important information to overcome my fear and help me make my decision to be a transplant donor. May God bless you with continued good health.

I also want to thank my caregivers; Jessie, my mother, Maria, my sister-in-law and my dear friend; Debbie. You all showed me so much love and care while re-cooperating after surgery. Thank you for taking the time to nurse me back to health, you all made me feel so loved and comforted. Love you so much.

To Nardy, Kim, and my daughter Jessica: Thank you for proofreading my book, and giving me editing advice and Godly wisdom.

To Jean-Marie: Thank you for taking time out of your busy life to encourage me about self- publishing.

To Jill: Thank you for proofreading my book several times and for giving me editing advice, moral support and encouragement on the completion of my book.

To Rachelle: Thank you for helping with the computer. You always made it so easy.

Preface

Painful Tears of Joy will take you on my personal journey of miracles. These miracles of God's faithfulness only came through hardships and trials. You can choose to melt while in the fire and suffer from fear, doubt, worry, anxiety, and depression, or you can rest in the Lord knowing He has your life in His hands.

You will come to a new depth of understanding the truth, that is written from the Bible, the one and only Book that will truly set you free; restore your peace and give you direction and hope for your life. The Holy Spirit which is the third person of the Trinity will bring you comfort and grace which is the ability to walk through the fire with victory. Remember, you are not alone, He will walk by your side as you face these difficult times. Allow the Holy Spirit to change you and shape you into what He wills for your life. The decision is totally up to you. *"See, I set before you today life and prosperity, death and destruction. For I command you today to love the Lord your God, to walk in His ways, and to keep His commands, decrees and laws; then you will live and increase, and the Lord your God will bless you in the land you are entering to possess"* (Deuteronomy 30:15-16).

Notice this scripture? He gives us two options to choose from, "life and prosperity" or "death and destruction." He gives us a command to love the Lord your God, to walk in His ways and to keep His commands. His ways would be to choose life and prosperity, and then His promise follows, that He will bless you. Don't feel discouraged, take heart, God's grace will carry you.

Introduction

Have you ever felt like giving up on life? What would you do if everything failed and there were no answers? Who would you hold on to if you felt like you lost all hope for your future? Would you feel forsaken by God? Have you ever felt like you're on a roller coaster that is going so fast it feels like you're out of control? Life has its painful and joyful experiences which can cause your emotions to tailspin. Painful circumstances can make you feel beaten down which can bring you to the point of feeling like life has ended or that joy may never become a reality.

I am Living Proof, that when you come to the end of yourself when this physical world no longer has any answers, Christ is your answer! He is your hope in hopeless and desperate situations. The pages in this book will reveal to you that you can walk in victory despite any negative situation. I will share my stories with you and valuable lessons I have learned while walking by faith and not by sight. I pray these testimonies of God's grace and miracles will encourage you to continue to have faith and believe for yours.

You will discover how your heart toward God and your obedient spirit can make a difference in how you view your sufferings, which truly is the attitude of the heart. God desires to shape you into what He wills for your life which comes from trust, faith, obedience, hope, perseverance, endurance, patience and longsuffering.

This message I share will bring hope as you learn to trust in the Messiah, whose name is Jesus. He is the Prince of Peace. He will fill you with joy in the midst of the darkest hour. You *can* rejoice in your sufferings. I pray as you read my testimonies you will be blessed and encouraged personally.

"May the God of hope fill you with all joy and peace as you trust in Him so that you may overflow with hope by the power of the Holy Spirit" (Romans 15:13).

CHAPTER 1

He Guides My Steps

God, do You really guide my steps? How can these steps be of You? I know the Bible says, "The steps of the righteous are ordered of God", but are they really? How can this path I'm walking be ordered of You? My road is dark, my path is dim and my steps are shattered. This road before me may cause me to stumble and lose my way. As I think about the steps before me and reflect on my path that I have walked, even though there have been many bumps in the road, I can see how You have guided me, even the moment I was born on December 13, 1963.

My birth was filled with complications, due to the doctor giving my mother too much anesthesia. It made my lungs very weak, and I had difficulty breathing; two days after my birth my mother was able to see me. When she was finally able to bring me home, I turned blue from loss of oxygen. Two weeks later, my health improved and I was dedicated in Smithtown Gospel Tabernacle, by our former pastor, Maurice Anderson.

I had several near death experiences growing up. My great grandmother was taking an afternoon nap at my parents' house; when she was awakened by a faint voice crying out for help. She immediately jumped out of bed, ran down the hallway, screamed for my parents that there was something wrong in the backyard.

My father, who is a large man and six foot two, went running outside and saw me hanging on the slide by my brother's Batman cape. As I was about to take my last breath, my father ran to my rescue and immediately lifted me from the slide and untied the cape that was around my neck; he destroyed the cape, and I'm here to tell the story.

I had pneumonia several times due to my weak lungs and at the age of nine, I had to be hospitalized. Twice, I almost drowned at Smiths Point which is an ocean with tremendously high waves. Thank God, other than those incidents I had a wonderful childhood, with no cares in the world. All my needs were met on a daily basis and beyond.

I have many happy memories of my childhood in church. I attended Sunday school every Sunday and was taught the Word of God. At the age of fourteen, I decided to be water baptized. Although I loved God and made my public confession to serve Him, I was curious and wanted to know what the world had to offer. I was not a leader as a teenager and was living a lifestyle that was edifying my flesh rather than obeying God. I witnessed to my friends while engaging in the same negative behaviors, and invited them to church and on youth retreats. After we would come home from church activities, we would begin the same lifestyle as before with little change.

Occasionally, as I got older, I would go to the town bar with a friend but never felt comfortable. I would walk over to a person who was sitting alone, strike up a conversation and invite them to church to tell them about Jesus. As you could see, I was living a double life.

I will never forget the time I was on a dance floor and heard God's voice say clearly, "If you don't get off this floor now, you never will." It was evident it was the voice of God. I immediately got off the floor and told my friend I had to go. I was miserable because I wanted to do what I thought was fun, but always heard God's usual voice in the back of my mind. I felt empty after several relationships ended. I was living a destructive lifestyle; half in church and half in the world for my own pleasure. I was making wrong choices that had no future for my life in a positive way. I decided to stop everything I was doing that was wrong and disobedient activities in the sight of God, but I could not quit smoking. I started at a young age, and believe it or not, it was a girl from church who introduced me to cigarettes. Watch your children, even in church.

For many years, I tried to live a Christian life but had no power to resist temptation. I always gave in, and then carried the guilt. I knew I needed to repent and change but didn't have any strength. God knew my heart and that was to please Him.

I remember questioning my mother and saying, "Mom, what happens if there is no God, how do you know?" She would always gently say, "You know, Debbie, that's a great question. If you lived your whole life serving God and He didn't exist, you've lost nothing. However, if you didn't serve God and He did exist, you lost everything." Simple, but it really made me think.

3

I had a longing to go back to youth camp because I remembered the feeling I got when I was in the presence of God. However, I was now past that age and there was nothing like that for me. One day I heard about Creation '82, and I knew I wanted to go. It didn't bother me that I barely knew the people who were going; I just knew I wanted to go. I signed up and went on a weekend trip to Pennsylvania. Creation is like a huge "Wood Stock," although this is Christian. Thousands of people from all over the country are listening to hundreds of musicians and great speakers from all over the world.

At Creation, I didn't bring any cigarettes with me because I was trying to quit, and I didn't want to smoke in front of God's people. I did have respect for that, but unfortunately, someone else had a pack with them so I asked for one. As I sat on a log smoking and watched others swim in the lake, the familiar voice that I heard in the past came into my mind and said, "Do you like when people commit suicide?" I thought, "Oh no! I don't!" Then I heard, "That is exactly what you're doing, only in a slow fashion." I put the cigarette down, asked God for help, and He delivered me twenty-two years ago.

The small inner voice that was with me all those years was the voice of the Holy Spirit who dwells in us.

Even When We Do Wrong, He's There To Guide You. Listen For That Soft, Gentle, and Peaceful Voice; He Will Speak To You Too.

The last night I was at Creation '82, I went to an outdoor meeting and heard a speaker preaching a sermon on living life without compromise. That one sermon made a dramatic change in my heart, and from that day forward, I made a commitment to live one hundred percent for Jesus. I was finished and wanted no part of being a hypocrite and playing church. I know all about acting one way during the week and another in church. I thought I was fooling everyone, but you can never fool God . . . or a praying mother.

After rededicating my life to Jesus, I felt as though I was all alone. It was God who I clung to; He became my best friend. I learned to put my trust, confidence and my life in His hands. How many times do we as Christians say, "Yes Lord, I give You my life, I trust You with my life. Use me in any way You can, I'm Yours." It is a process of dying to yourself until your desires become His. All I wanted to do was learn about Jesus. I was not the typical eight-teen-year-old; it was just the Lord and me. It was as if I was placed in a cocoon that was silent and isolated from the world; waiting to burst out and become who I was intended to be.

There were times, I was tempted by phone calls from friends who wanted to engage in the same activities, but I knew I didn't want to continue in the same old ways and had to stand for what I believed. I wanted to be changed and finally, it happened! I was able to stand for what I believed; it didn't matter if I was alone!

5

A few months after Creation, I was in an evening church service and received the baptism of the Holy Spirit. I will never forget that evening service. I went up to the altar and had an altar worker pray over me. I knew something mighty and different had occurred. The joy that flooded my soul was an amazing unspeakable joy that I had never experienced. I was delivered! I no longer had any desire to continue anything I was once engaged in. After that experience, when I went to church, I never needed to go to the altar in repentance of the same thing. When there was an altar call, I checked my heart and knew I was able to stand in the presence of God clean.

Not because of whom I was, but because of His grace and the power to resist the temptations that once had a hold on me.

When I was nineteen, I attended Bible class for one year on Monday evenings. Eventually, Monday classes were not enough for me; I had a hunger to learn more about Jesus. I began attending Tuesday night meetings at Christ For The Nations Bible Institute in Stony Brook, Long Island. I was so impressed to see other young people who had a love for God and the Truth as much as I did. I began going to Christ For The Nations every Tuesday night for meetings and during the day to other classes; although I was not enrolled as a student.

One Tuesday night, while at the service, a young woman came to me with excitement and told me how I should become a student. I couldn't believe she was telling me this because I knew the Lord was knocking on my heart, but fear of the unknown was also knocking.

When I went home that evening, I thought about what occurred and made plans to go back to speak to the dean of women to become a student. I knew without a shadow of a doubt I was to be at that school. I spoke to Sister Willie, a beautiful older woman who was so kind and gentle and explained my situation.

I already planned to go on a trip to Israel with Smithtown Gospel Tabernacle Church. I explained that when I returned I wanted to be enrolled as a student. She began to tell me I wasn't able to start in the middle of the semester. Enrollment began in January, and I had to either enroll then or wait until the following semester. After praying, I decided to change my plans to go to Israel, and go to Christ For The Nations. I knew that was where the Lord wanted me to be, and I wanted to be obedient.

I brought my mother to show her what I wanted to do, and at the age of twenty-one, I enrolled as a student. I experienced the presence of God in a new and powerful way. This new life of being a Christian college student was filled with learning the Bible and all of God's miracles. I didn't always have that desire, it began at around age eighteen. I was an extremely different twenty-one-year-old girl.

I wasn't involved in the "normal" things of life like looking for a mate. The Lord laid it specifically on my heart that I was only to concentrate on Him. I was focused on this mission that was placed before me. I'm not going to lie, I was afraid; somehow, I never let my fears control what I did.

Bible school was a different experience; I learned how to not only build a stronger relationship with God but to build relationships with people. We all have weaknesses of some sort or another; mine was the fear of people. I'm going, to be honest with you and expose many of my own weaknesses to show you how to gain the victory and overcome. I was afraid of people getting too close and finding out who I really was. Not smart enough, not funny enough, maybe I would say the wrong thing, this was because I was insecure. All I wanted was Jesus, but when it came to friendships I isolated myself. I felt as though people weren't accepting me for who I was. Fear gripped me and I had to fight against the feelings of insecurity to learn how to make myself vulnerable; so I would be able to build relationships.

When I finally began to make friends, and they did accept me, I realized everything I was feeling wasn't the truth. I opened up to my roommate one night and told her how I was feeling. She laughed and laughed because she couldn't believe I felt that way. She told me how she saw me as someone who had it all together.

Negative thoughts can prevent you from what God has for you if you allow it. What's amazing is, no one knew what I was going through; people can look like they have it all together on the outside but are hurting within. Even though I was afraid, I was able to push through those walls and begin to make lasting friendships. Friendships, that were real, and who accepted me for who I was.

Bible school was exciting; there were times when classes were cancelled because the power of God was evident. People were weeping before Him and being healed of past hurts, or some were just praising Him.

The classes were intense, especially Spiritual Warfare and Christ the Healer; my favorite topics. I learned so much truth and insight and had a deep desire to be used of God in the healing ministry. That simply means to pray for the sick and see them recover. The Christ the Healer class taught me about what Jesus did for us on the cross which I simply believed by faith, and it became a living reality in my heart. I'm going to share some of it with you.

What Jesus Did For Us On The Cross Is Twofold.

I would like to explain what I mean by this expression. *"Everyone who calls upon the name of the Lord will be saved" (Romans 10:13).*

The word "saved" is the same word used in the book of Mark when He said, "as many (sick) people touched Him were "made whole" (Mark 6:56; KJ). Both words "saved" and "made whole" were translated from the Greek word Sozo which refers to healing both spiritually and physically.

Think about the story of the man who was paralyzed, Jesus said, *"Which is easier: to say to this paralyzed man 'Your sins are forgiven'; or to say 'Get up, take your mat and walk?"* *(Mark 2:9-12, NIV).* This paralyzed man the Bible speaks about had a desperate situation. He had friends who loved and cared about him so much they went the extra mile to see him healed. The crowd was so large and the house too packed that they made a hole in the roof and brought their friend to Jesus. Notice, when Jesus saw their faith, He said to the paralyzed man, "Your sins are forgiven" and then He said, "I tell you, get up, take your mat and go home." (Twofold)

He Simply Listened To The Command Of God
"He got up, took his mat and walked out in full view of everyone." He was forgiven of his sins and healed in his body. He was a clean new man, inside and out! I can just picture everyone's mouth drop open with amazement! The Bible says, "This amazed everyone, and the result was they praised God."

This story reminds me of many of us. We may not be paralyzed in our body, but we may be crippled in our thinking, emotions, and fears. It's not until the Word, the Bible, becomes real in our hearts that we can be set free. It's no longer head knowledge (Logos), but heart knowledge, (Rhema). Don't allow yourself to stay crippled for thirty years or even thirty days, or minutes. Arise in Jesus' Name. "You are healed by His stripes". By the blood, He shed for you at Calvary.

The First Benefit We Receive At Salvation Is The Forgiveness Of Sins.

The word "salvation" means to **"deliver, protect and to heal."** Salvation includes **redemption for the whole man; body, soul and spirit.** We are a three part human just as the God Head is a three part deity. God the Father, God the Son, and God the Holy Spirit. Jesus came to earth in a body, the Spirit helps us with our emotions which is our soul and God is Spirit. *"Those who worship Him must worship Him in Spirit and truth"* (John 4:24).

Healing Is Also Included In The First Benefit.

When you hear me say, "He was pierced for our transgressions and crushed (wounded) for our iniquity." I'm speaking of spiritual healing and the forgiveness of sins. "The punishment (chastisement) of our peace was upon Him" speaks of emotional healing for your mind and soul which is your emotions. "By His wounds (stripes) you are healed" speaks of healing for your body. He took those beatings for us. Notice, it is present tense, you "are" healed, not "you may be" or "you will be."

Jesus was whipped thirty-nine times. Every time the whip pulled His skin back, it tore pieces of flesh right off His body. He did this for you and me so we would be totally set free (Isaiah 53:5).

As you can see, what I was taught was very deep and full of wisdom and truth.

I kept it close to my heart and continued my education.

CHAPTER 2

Saving Grace

After my first semester of school, during the summer, I decided to go to Mexico for one month on my first mission experience. Before I left for my trip, I had visions of flashing lights before me and had the feeling of death. I would envision ambulances in front of my home. I thought the Lord was trying to tell me something about my trip. As these warnings continued, I realized it was for my father. I talked to my brother and mother one morning as we sat around the kitchen table and prayed for my father's safety. About three weeks later, I left for Mexico with, Youth with the Mission. (An organization that assists the poor and shares the gospel).

Mexico was great! We went to local parks to perform drama, handed out Bibles door to door, visited the local orphanage where there were so many children waiting to be adopted. They were so happy to receive bubbles and a small child's book about Jesus. We had such a wonderful time loving and praying for the people. It is extremely different from America, people were so happy to receive the Lord and grateful to receive a Bible. When we went door to door in their neighborhood, they invited us into their home and began serving us soda while we talked to them about God. They were also so full of joy taking care of their house, even if they were sweeping a dirt walkway that led to their small home.

One morning, while outside enjoying the view from the mountain where we were living, I began to have thoughts of my father. I knew something was wrong and prayed for his safety and protection. I had no idea around the same time I began to pray, back at home in Long Island, my father suffered from a severe car accident that could have been fatal. On the way home from Mexico, I stopped off at Texas to visit my relatives and then after a few days arrived home.

When I came home from my long trip, only my brother picked me up from the airport. I thought that was a little strange since I had been gone for five weeks. As we approached the car, I noticed my mother sitting in it. She was happy to see me, but I could feel something was wrong, and I wondered where dad was. As we left the airport and were driving home, my brother pulled over to the side of the road, turned around because I was sitting in the back seat and took my hand. "My heart was beating so fast," he then began to tell me that our dad had been in a severe car accident. He was dragged and run over by a car while changing a flat tire on 347 which is the main highway where we live.

My mother was on her way to work and was delayed in traffic due to the accident. She had no idea it was her husband lying on the street being cared for by the paramedics. As she approached the car, she turned to look and realized it was her husband. She pulled over, ran to the police and told them she was his wife. My mother worked at a hospital and when they brought him to the emergency room, the word was out that an employee's husband was badly injured. Thank God the best doctor was available to perform the surgery. He had heart contusions and was extremely hurt. His leg was shattered below his knee and they didn't think he would be able to walk.

Father's Car Accident

After they broke the news to me we drove to the hospital to see my father that very day. When we got to the hospital he was being moved out of ICU to a new room. He came home after seven weeks of being in the hospital with fifteen metal pins in his leg to keep it together. During this time, the doctor was concerned that he had no bone growth in his leg, which meant he may have to have it amputated. Eight months later, bone growth began to appear and his leg and life was spared, praise God!

Two months after my father's car accident, the second semester of school began. The director came in to talk to all the students to let us know the program had become a two-year school, and if anyone wanted to stay on they could. I was so thrilled about this opportunity so I decided to stay and continue my education. During our first semester of the second year, they also added a third year. My classmates had started in September so they were asked to complete an internship at their local church. I had one more semester to complete to finish my second year and that is when the new guy on campus arrived.

One day before chapel, one of our friends introduced Joey to all of us. We were all in the same evangelism class and Joe and I were also in the same tribe group which is a small prayer group. He was always in the library studying and occasionally we went with a group of friends for ice cream. One other time, we went to the city with two friends and met a man who was addicted to drugs. He wanted to change his life and needed a rehabilitation program. After making a phone call to a particular program, we brought this young man to the center and enjoyed the day.

After completing my second year, I enjoyed my summer, then began my third-year internship with Christ For The Nations; which was to complete three months overseas.

I chose to go to Guatemala because I love the Hispanic people. I went with six other classmates to work alongside missionaries who worked for Living Water Teaching. Several missionary children lived on campus, so we were able to encourage them as well as help to build a church.

One of the most precious memories I have is when I was asked to speak in a women's prison. I don't speak Spanish, but thankfully I had a translator. Most of the women were in for prostitution or drug-related charges. The prison allowed the women to care for their young children while incarcerated; it was so touching to see such young children living with their mothers in prison.

Hospital visits were made every day with a special missionary woman named Julie, who visited and prayed for the sick. We visited schools and performed drama for the children at an orphanage as well as play basketball to bring smiles on their precious faces.

What a beautiful time of learning and experiencing life in another country.

Living in the jungle in order to assist the people of a particular village was a major highlight. A dentist was brought in to serve people with tooth decay and pulled over five hundred teeth in five days. We also provided vitamins, food, Bibles and teachings about hygiene. Talk about hygiene, every day several women came to the campus with jugs of water being carried on their head. One cup of water was provided for us per day, to use to drink, bathe, or brush our teeth! That was it for the day! You can only imagination how it was used! I'm glad I have the personality who can adapt to any situation.

What really made an impression on me was a woman walking up a steep road barefoot. She was carrying a stack of wood on her head, a basket of food in her arm and baby on her back wrapped in a cloth sling. Can you imagine the strength this woman had? It was definitely incredible. Seeing this truly made me grateful for where I lived.

When I came home from Guatemala, I was allowed to graduate in May with my classmates; with the stipulation, I would complete my three months internship at my local church. (The picture you see is of my graduation with Joe in 1987. We were friends and had no idea what the future held).

Joe and I at Graduation

The duties I was given as an intern at church, was to teach Sunday school, go with Pastor Robert Forseth (the former senior pastor of Smithtown Gospel Tabernacle) to the hospitals to pray for the sick, visit certain shut-ins (which I loved), and I always had a heart for prison ministry, so I was blessed to accompany pastor John Arntsen who was the leader of the prison ministry. I also helped with some paperwork in the church office. After, I finally completed the internship I was now ready to receive my diploma in Biblical Studies and Christian Leadership and began working at a counseling center as a receptionist.

Even though I had a job, I was not satisfied and thought about the drama I learned while in Mexico and Guatemala. I made an appointment to speak with Pastor Forseth and with his permission; I put a team together from church. Every Friday night, a group of us met together and I taught the skits I learned while on the mission field. After we felt confident, I called the Bowery Mission, and we were invited to go there to perform drama in the evening service.

When we arrived, we were directed to go to the kitchen to make sandwiches, and then we were sent to Tompkins Square Park to help another ministry called, Hope For The Future. We were placed behind a table to serve food to about eight hundred individuals. There were hundreds of people and many different nationalities, I felt as though I was on the mission field right in my own backyard. It was truly shocking to see hundreds of homeless and destitute people, totally depending on this ministry to eat that afternoon.

In the evening, we went to a service with the Bowery Mission to perform our drama. Before we went in the building flyers for the event were handed out to the people on the street. My friend and I met a young woman who we began to talk to. She had many issues that happened in her life and was really in need of help. Before the service, we took her to the nearest grocery store and bought food and toiletries to bless her with.

After the service when saying good-bye, I heard the soft, gentle familiar voice of the Holy Spirit; who told me to give away my Bible. I placed it near my heart and didn't want to let it go.

This Bible was so precious to me, because it went to Bible school, on the mission field, had so many notes and scriptures highlighted that I loved and many memories of all the places we traveled together.

As we were leaving, I had to listen to and be obedient to the prompting of the Holy Spirit. I told this woman, I wanted her to have my Bible, and she began to cry. She refused at first, but when I explained what had taken place and that it was God who wanted her to have it; she took it with a huge smile on her face. We kept in touch for a while and she did begin going to church and changing her life.

During the evening, I couldn't get the experience out of my mind. I called Pastor Diane from Hope For The Future and began volunteering every Monday and Friday evenings as well as all day Saturday. I had a strong desire to be used of God. In fact, I came across a letter I wrote to the Lord and I will share a portion of it.

"Father, continue to break my heart and teach me to walk by faith. Teach me by your Spirit. Give me discernment, knowledge, and understanding. I choose to be obedient, lead and guide me. My Abba Father, I trust You, I know You will supply my every need."

As you continue to read my story, you will see how that prayer has been and is still being granted. ***"Teach me, to walk by faith."***

CHAPTER 3

My Prayer

I was single and twenty-four when I began volunteering for Hope For The Future Ministry. My mother would occasionally say to me, "Debbie isn't there anyone you want to marry?" "Does God have to bring him down from Heaven?" I sat on my bed and told her, "If there was anyone I would want to marry, it would be Joey because I love his heart, but I don't know." What I meant by "I love his heart" was the purity in it, his love, zeal and passion for God, outweighed anything I had ever noticed in a man. I had a desire to be married, but I didn't know if God was calling me to be single. I wondered why God placed me in a ministry with several single women.

One night, after coming home from a long day, I decided to say a prayer and tape record it so I would be able to see how God answered me. I'd like to share it with you. Let's go back to March 1, 1988. That night was a very special evening, I still remember that night like it was yesterday.

I was alone in my room with my small, pocket tape recorder. Many of you who are reading this book probably have never seen a tape recorder or have even heard of one; however, it worked! I'm going to highlight certain words or phrases in my prayer so you will be able to study them and keep them deep in your heart like I have.

My Prayer Begins

"Father, I bring You the desires of my heart. I pray that You would **hear my cry** and, **by faith,** it would be fulfilled. **I give You** my life, my soul, and everything within me. I pray You would **anoint me** in Jesus' Name, and Your anointing would flow within me. I have written down on paper all that You have shown me, and I would like to put it on tape so I can **look back** and see, how You, Lord, have worked in my life.

I pray I would **truly consider others better than myself**. Help me to have a **servant's heart;** that I would learn to **serve not for anything in return**. Never look at others, but **keep my eyes totally on You.** I've seen in the past that when I get my eyes off You Lord and put them on people, **people will fail**, they are human. The only one who will **never fail is You, Lord Jesus.**

I've noticed that in the past couple of months, I've been wanting to compromise, but, I know I have a high calling on my life and I'm going to keep my standards high. **You have chosen me and called me. I have a special ministry to fulfill.** I will keep in mind **that I am, chosen, redeemed, cleansed, righteous and royal; I'm a child of the King.**

Father, I give You my life, **I trust You** with my life. You have never let me down so why should You start now. **You**

are faithful. I know You haven't forgotten me, but You see me and You are still working on and in me.

I pray for my life, I have such a deep desire to serve You. I love You; move in and through my life. **Cause me to be a light, cause me to proclaim the gospel, fill my mouth, and anoint me.** I pray for a special touch from Heaven.

I lift up my husband to You, I pray wherever he may be, that You touch him with the **spirit of praise instead of heaviness;** and love, peace, and joy. I pray for a deep desire to **serve You.** He must be **in love with You, Jesus.**

Father, I pray You **purify** him and **refine** him. I pray for **character building,** that he feel so lost around everyone, he falls on his knees to You. **Break him, shape him, mold him, fill him,** and then **use him.**

Fill him with the Spirit of God intensely, and **wisdom, discernment, knowledge,** and **understanding.** Open his eyes, give him revelation, and teach him to be a man of his word. Give him **compassion,** break him and purify him into the man You want him to be. **He's out of the world but cause the world to be out of him.** **Renew his mind,** enable him to be filled with authority **knowing his position**. I pray for **leadership qualities,** administration qualities build them within him. I pray he learn to be **responsible**, have a **dependency on You, Jesus.** That he would not run from responsibility but face it with confidence and trust in You. That he would learn to **trust in You** for everything.

I pray for his finances, that You, God, would bless it; that he would learn to have a **giving heart**. I pray for his job that You would open the doors and he would find **favor with man**, but if he is called to the full-time ministry he would **submit to Your will**.

I pray for a **submissive heart, a yielded hear**t toward You. He must **love his wife as Christ loved the church,** a man in love with one woman; love her as his own, as if she were taken right from his own side. He must not mind if I desire to be in the ministry, knowing **our home comes first.**

I pray for **integrity, honesty, the** character of a lamb, **gentle, meek** and **humble** and a lion, **bold, stern and strong.** He must be the protector, intelligent in the things of the world and of God. Take away all pride and disrespect.

I pray he learn to **honor others above himself,** he must be **balanced** in his attitude of thinking not leaning too much on one side, he must have an open heart, a good listener and talkative. He must be **sensitive to the needs of others** having a desire to help and understand.

I pray our spirits would mesh together, that we would be one in the spirit and in body. He must have a fear of You, respect, and reverence. He must love people but must learn the **character of a Godly man.** How does a Godly man show himself, especially around women! He must have his shield up at all times the enemy is very sly. He must be a **family man** desiring to be the man of the home, believes in correction, discipline, and love.

I desire to have a home where it can be my husband's resting place, a haven, where peace reigns because God rules. Where people can come for healing; healing of

emotions, and where **prayer is a big part of our home.**
I desire to open my home to less fortunate people, to
clothe the naked, to give someone a cup of water in
Jesus' Name. I desire to reach out to the lost and hurting
with my husband. He must be the **spiritual leader;** I
must be **protected** under him. Fill him with the gifts
of the spirit, teaching, healing etc. He must be a man of
commitment, raise him up, Jesus, prepare him even
now, and show him how to take on **responsibility.** I bind
all fear in Jesus Name, Thank You Lord Amen!

Thank You, Jesus, that You hear my prayers, that You
will fulfill my prayers. I know You are raising him up
even now. I thank You Lord that the things he is going
through right now are building character in him; I praise
You, God, for a godly man.

Thank You, Father, that You have that someone special
for me in my life. I thank You that we will work together
for Your Kingdom. Thank You, for the anointing You will
place upon us. Let Your Spirit go forth and prepare us
together right now, even though we don't know who we
are yet. I pray that Your Holy Spirit will go forth and
prepare us for the great and mighty things that You have.

That prayer was prayed one year after I graduated
from Christ For The Nations Bible Institute. I never knew
I was praying for Joe even though we knew each other.
When I read that prayer to him and told him he was
everything I prayed for, he said, as he laughed, "Now I
know why I was going through all those hard places."

Truly, he was encouraged that I would think of him like that.

I encourage anyone to pray that prayer if you are single, or even married. I have to say, God answered every point I made. What's interesting is, I never prayed for my husband's health. We both find that extremely interesting, it never crossed my mind. If you notice, I only prayed for his character.

In today's world, it's about looks, wealth, and prestige. Looks will fade, you can lose your money and job in an instant, but your character and who you are will remain. God blessed me with everything I prayed for and more.

CHAPTER 4

My Gift

After I graduated Christ For The Nations, Joe continued his education to complete his three years of training in Biblical studies and chose to go to Spain for his internship. He was asked to be the team leader and was able to really learn firsthand about leadership.

A few months after I graduated school, I was home and received a phone call from a friend of my mother. She explained to me when she was in prayer, the Lord placed it on her heart to take me to Israel, all expenses paid! Can you believe it? I had given up my trip to go to Bible School and the Lord laid it on Franc's heart to take me to Israel all expenses paid! I always had a desire to go to Israel, and now, God had given me my heart's desire. I thought of it as my graduation gift from the Lord. I was so excited to know I was on my way to Israel.

When we arrived, we drove to King David's Hotel, which was on top of the Mt. of Olives overlooking Jerusalem. It was so amazing to walk the places I read about in the Bible. When we went to the town of Jerusalem, you could see Golgotha, "The place of the skull" up on a hill in the middle of town, where Jesus hung on the cross to bleed and die. Just to think, His blood and death were our gift of life.

When I went to Bible school, I learned all about the blood of Jesus in the class "Christ the Healer." It might sound a little awkward to talk about the blood of Christ, but there is power in it. The blood is what washes clean, it purifies and makes new. The blood is the only thing that can wash away our sin and reconcile us back to God, and remove our guilt and shame. There is no forgiveness of sins without the shedding of blood. This is the key to great healing whether it is body, mind, or spirit.

The custom in Jerusalem many centuries ago was to sacrifice a lamb or goat for sin. Thank God, we no longer have to do that, because Jesus, the Messiah, became our ultimate sacrificial Lamb of God who took away the sins of the whole world. He is our atonement. *"When Christ came as high priest of the good things that are already here, He went through the greater and more perfect tabernacle, that is not man- made, that is to say, not a part of creation. He did not enter by means of the blood of goats and calves, but He entered the most Holy Place once and for all by His own blood, having obtained eternal redemption. The blood of goats and bulls and ashes of a heifer sprinkled on those who were ceremonially unclean sanctify them so that they are outwardly clean, how much more, then will the blood of Christ, who through the eternal Spirit offered Himself unblemished to God, cleanse our conscience from acts that lead to death, so that we may serve the living God" (Hebrews 9:11-14).*

I Have Learned This Truth So Many Years Ago; Which Has Truly Been My Saving Grace Through Life.

While in the garden, visiting the tomb, where Jesus was buried and resurrected, I heard people singing the song, *"Because He lives I can face tomorrow"* in their native language, it was such a precious moment. I went to Israel when they were celebrating the Feast of Tabernacle. "The Feast of Tabernacles is a Jewish festival celebrating the harvest and remembering when the Jews wandered in the wilderness after they exited Egypt." Thousands of Christians from all over the world were there to celebrate that special occasion. One morning, we all marched from the Mt. of Olives to Mt. Zion singing and holding our flag to represent our country. I was also able to take a boat ride on the Sea of Galilee and was baptized for the second time in the Jordan River, which was so exciting to know I was baptized in the same river as my Lord.

I also had the opportunity to sit in on a service from Gwen Shaw, the author of the devotional I use in this book. Whoever knew, years later, the words she penned would make such a profound impact on my life; through every trial, I would go through in the years ahead.

One beautiful morning, I had just come out of the hotel and felt like I was going to do something different that day. I was standing by the rock wall overlooking Jerusalem, a car with a large family came out and was also enjoying the view. I struck up a conversation with this precious Muslim family and they invited me to their home. Back then, I had no fear of experiencing life and jumped in the car and went. It was so much fun being in their home, laughing, eating and trying to communicate. God is good!

When I think about this whole trip, God blessed me, because of my obedience to Him. Isn't it wonderful how the Lord uses us as His hands? If Fran wasn't obedient that would have prevented me from receiving my miracle. Francs' miracle came from my mother who worked with her for many years. She was exploring witchcraft and the Lord used my mother to invite her to church where she gave her life to Jesus; which is truly wonderful being she was Jewish. She then quit her job and worked full time for the Lord until He called her home.

Fran is the one who gave me the devotional I use many times in this book. I pray these passages from the devotional _Day by Day a Daily Praise Offering_ from Gwen Shaw will bless you as much as they have blessed me. She is truly a blessing and a handmaiden of the Lord. Always be open and ready to be used of God. The Bible does say: *"Give and it shall be given unto you. A good measure, pressed down, and shaken together and running over, will be poured into your lap. For with the measure you use, it will be the measured to you"* (Luke 6:38).

When you are willing to be obedient to the Lord, He will do for you and surprise you with good things. He wants to bless His children; He wants to provide for His children. As you continue to read, you will witness miracle after miracle, which comes from the provision of the Lord.

CHAPTER 5

❧

From Miracle to Miracle

After I returned from Israel, I continued working at the counseling agency and volunteering with Hope For The Future. Every Monday night at six o'clock we met a large group of homeless people at the subway stations, in the lower Eastside, of Manhattan to give them a hot meal, blankets, and prayer. We also drove around the neighborhood looking for squatters to provide them with food, blankets, and toiletries.

These individuals live in abandoned buildings and barely existed on a daily basis. They were most eager to receive our assistance since their life was one of meager possessions. They accepted our help and often times allowed us to pray for them which also gave us the chance to not only care for their physical needs but their spiritual needs as well.

My tasks at the ministry had very long late hours, we would get home around five in the morning when the birds were singing and I had to get ready to go to work for the day. During this time of working with the ministry I also worked at the counseling agency and I made sure I took my lunch break every Tuesday. On this particular break, I decided to read my Bible; it was as if God spoke directly to me. It read, *"That servant who knows his master's will and does not get ready or does not do what his master wants will be beaten with many blows. But, the one who does not know and does things deserving punishment will be beaten with few blows.*

From everyone who has been given much, much is demanded; and from the one who has been entrusted with much, much more will be asked" (Luke 12:47).

I immediately closed my Bible and knew what to do. I had to be obedient to God and I gave my two weeks' notice at the counseling agency that very day to work full time with Pastor Diane at Hope For The Future Ministry. I was so excited about being involved in full-time ministry advocating for the homeless. I loved going on the streets of Manhattan to minister to the hurting people; it consumed my every thought. It was no longer just Monday nights, Fridays and Saturdays, I was now volunteering five days a week. It was hard work, but the rewards were great. The rewards were eternal; people's lives were being transformed and set free from addictions, phobias, and lifestyles that were destroying their lives.

One night before I went out to volunteer, my mother told me she was impressed with dreams for many nights of a flashing sign saying, "danger." She told me about her dream, but I didn't want to hear what she had to say, I knew she had some fear of me working on the streets of New York City in the middle of the night. I couldn't understand why she felt that way! She always said to me, "Debbie, even pastors are home in bed," but I didn't care,

I knew this is what God wanted me to do, and also, what I wanted to do. My attitude was "Mom, this is what I'm doing and I don't want to hear it."

Ouch! I realize now that wasn't the way to handle that situation and it was an extremely harsh attitude.

This particular Friday night, my mother didn't want to go to bed until I was home. She sat in the living room waiting for me, when all of a sudden, she heard an explosion.

A few minutes later the doorbell rang and it was her neighbors, Tom, and his mom, crying as they said, "Debbie has been in a car accident." My parents rushed to get in the car, drove down to the end of the block and saw my crushed car. There were several fire trucks and ambulances there at the scene and the fire department was trying to get me out of the car. They were surprised my car didn't blow up since the gas tank was hit. I was told, that all my neighbors didn't think I was going to survive. The paramedics were about to put a trachea down my throat because I couldn't breathe when I vomited and it cleared my passage way.

My Car Accident

I don't remember anything except thinking about how I had to give myself a manicure for the wedding I was in the next day. Right before I made my turn to enter the street I lived on, I looked in my rearview mirror and saw a huge truck behind me. As I was turning left onto my street, a huge Chevy pickup with balloon tires tried to go around me from the left. The truck smashed into the back end of my car and driver's side, ran over my car and flipped over. My mother's neighbors were up and heard the screech of the cars before they even hit and called 911. I was told the person who hit me had a 2.4 level of alcohol, which means he was doubly intoxicated. He also had no registration, no license, and no insurance.

When I arrived at the hospital, they immediately sewed twenty-seven stitches in my head and a little while later, the nurse came to my mother, sister-in-law, and Pastor Greco and asked, "Does your daughter speak Greek or Latin?" They weren't sure what the nurse meant until they realized, it was the Holy Spirit that was speaking through me. The Holy Spirit, who I was listening to all those years, was praying for me and through me while I was unconscious! I still can't get over that! He is so mighty and powerful! Praise the Living God!

"In the same way, the Spirit helps us in our weakness. We do not know what we ought to pray for, but the Spirit Himself intercedes for us with groans that words cannot express. And, He who searches our hearts knows the mind of the Spirit because the Spirit intercedes for the saints in accordance with God's will" (Romans 8:26-27).

Can You Imagine? Isn't That Awesome? The Spirit Prays For Us In Accordance To God's Will.

The will of God is to bring life and life more abundantly. He wants to give us "immeasurably more than we can think of or ask." The Word *"will"* means *testament.* In the Bible, we have the Old and the New Testament; promises from God. In Hebrews it reads, a will cannot go into effect until someone dies. *"In the case of a will, it is necessary to prove the death of the one who made it, because a will is in force only when somebody has died; it never takes effect while the one who made it is living"* (Hebrews 9:16-18). Jesus died on the cross, rose again and sent His Holy Spirit to us and is praying for us in accordance with

God's will, we can expect His promises to be fulfilled. Simple! His will and testament says, *"Beloved, I pray that you may be in good health and that all may go well with you, even as your soul is getting along well"* (3 John 2).

I woke up two days later, with a bright light over my head and a few doctors looking at me. They asked me if I knew where I was and I said, "No." They told me I was in the hospital, and that I was in a car accident, I immediately said, "Get me out of here! I have to be in my friend's wedding." They said, "Sorry honey, that was yesterday, you missed it." They were extremely happy to see I had no memory loss. I spent ten days in the hospital, it was so precious to see how many people really cared and loved me. My wall was covered with posters and cards from so many friends and family members. Praise God, He knows our hearts, and despite mine and the accident which was so horrific and devastating, He protected me, and spared my life. To God be the glory!

The day I came home from the hospital, I felt impressed to read my devotional, Day by Day, a Daily Praise Offering. It was now June 17, 1987; it was as if God came down from Heaven and sat right in front of me to say,

"I Have Delivered You So You Can Serve Me" (Psalm 71:20-24).

"Daughter, I have allowed you to experience great and painful troubles, and even troubles so great that it seemed as though they were going to destroy you. But you have learned many precious valuable lessons from these awful experiences. You thought they would kill you, and they would have if I hadn't stood by you to help you and save you and deliver you. And I have delivered you so that you might serve Me. I have brought you back from the depths of despair, even from what would have been your grave. I have moved on the hearts of evil men and bound up demon spirits that I might spare you from death before your time. Now I want to bring good out of your life, My child. I didn't save your life so you could go on living as you have in the past. I saved it so that I could make a child of God out of you. You shall become great with My greatness and not with the greatness of this world. I will comfort you by sharing your pain, your fears, and your travail. I will envelop you with My arms of love and help you forget all the horrors of the past and the sufferings of yesterday. Trust in Me and it shall be done, for I am greater than the most powerful, demonically controlled men."

Read the first couple of lines again, "You have learned many precious valuable lessons!" The Lord is so good and merciful. When I think about every trial I have gone through and am going through I can always see His faithfulness. He can spare you from death before your time. I have seen the provision of God ever since I gave my life to Him. Even though the road has been tough and full of trials, God has been faithful!

Another evening the doorbell rang again and this time it was a huge group of young pioneer girls from my church to sing for me. (Pioneer girls are just like girl scouts). It was so precious and they truly made me feel so loved. After a few months of recuperation, I went back to work full time in the ministry of Hope For The Future. Everyone was so joyful to welcome me back and was encouraged to hear of God's miraculous protection.

During this time I was volunteering with Hope For The Future and having a car accident, Joe continued his education at Christ For The Nations. I remember lying on my parent's bed talking to him on the phone telling him about my car accident. A few days later a gift arrived. It was a beautiful glass stained plaque that read,

"With God behind us and His arms beneath us, we can face whatever lies before us." Who ever knew years later those words would be something to live by for our marriage.

CHAPTER 6

❦

Our Romance Begins, Miracles Flow

While attending Christ For The Nations, Joe was able to sit in some English classes at Stony Brook University; although he didn't earn any credits because it was for free, the wisdom he gained was more valuable.

After he graduated Bible school, he had a desire to attend college to get a degree but had no idea where to go. In 1989 there were no cell phones, he stood on the corner of 24th and Park Avenue in Manhattan and called the directory to ask for information about finding universities in the area. To his surprise, there was the New York Theological Seminary five blocks from where he was.

On the seventh floor of this building, there was also a cell campus of the College of New Rochelle. For the next three years, we didn't see each other because he was very busy completing college. He finished a bachelor's degree in three years, with three majors and honors. I do brag about his success because that is a miracle in its self. When he was in high school, in the eleventh grade, a so-called "teacher" told him he should quit school and go to work. Joe believed the lie and never went back. Two years later, he earned his GED and it wasn't until he was twenty-eight when he read his first book. Going to Christ For The Nations was the most crucial life changing experience for Joe.

While going to college, he was employed by a home health care service and cared for a Jewish elderly couple. He took such good care of them, that the man told Joe, "You take better care of me than my own son." As he cared for this elderly man, Joe would tell him about the Messiah. One day, Simon told Joe he wanted to learn more about this "Jesus" and right before he died, he confessed Him as Lord. After this man died, Joe had to move on because he could not care for his wife alone. Before he did, he asked the Lord "How can Simon receive You and not his spouse?" After talking again with Mrs. P, she said to Joe, "Your God is my God and where you go I shall go too." This is the quote from the book of Ruth. Shortly after that, she passed away, and he was so thankful to have that opportunity.

During this time of going to college, Joe was also a leader at his church, the Vineyard Fellowship in Manhattan. He was the leader of a large prayer group that was soon to become his church branched off from the Vineyard in the Bronx. As you can see, he absolutely had no time for anyone. After my car accident, we went out once to dinner and the theater. He told me back then that he hoped we could build a deeper relationship, but I ran the other way. I told him "I can't say yes and I can't say no!" I didn't know how I felt and was so afraid of making a mistake. We laugh about that now, I have to say, I was very cautious. I was a very happy person, and didn't want anyone to ruin that!

For the next few years, we talked to each other occasionally on the phone and wrote letters to each other periodically. I ran into him once as he was coming out of a Christian bookstore in Queens. Another time he brought Bibles on the street to give to Hope For The Future ministry, so we were able to bless people with them. He was connected with the American Bible Association and they supplied him with grants to receive Bibles. He was volunteering his time at Lamb's Chapel that was located in midtown Manhattan (also feeding the homeless), as well as completing college and working.

One day I went to the mailbox and opened a letter from Joe. He sent me a picture of himself at graduation. When I saw it, I can't explain it, but it was almost shocking because God was giving me a deep love for him, yet I hadn't seen him in three years except for those few small brief encounters.

After he graduated from college, he made plans to go back to Spain for the second time to help the pastor he met during his Christ For The Nations internship. He wanted to help complete the Bible school that was erected in 1989. While Joe was there, the pastor asked him to stay and work with him. He explained there were many beautiful young single women who would love for him to remain working with their ministry. Joe didn't feel called to stay and told the pastor he had a two-way ticket and needed to go home.

God was placing a love in my heart for Joe while he was in Spain and he for me; yet, we didn't realize it; it really is amazing how the Lord put us together. We never dated; we were just friends from school. When Joe went to Spain for the second time, a thought crossed my mind, "What happens if he stays there?" His mother's family is originally from Spain and I knew how much he loved it there.

One evening I went to a graduation service from a rehabilitation program I supported. To my surprise, Joe's parents were sitting behind me at the next table. I said, "Hello," The only time I had met them was when I was a student at Christ For The Nations. We spoke for a few minutes and Joe's Mom, Teresa, told me, Joe was still in Spain.

On occasion, Joe and I wrote letters to each other to catch up with one another, I wrote him a letter to encourage him on the mission field. The letter went all the way to Spain, and he was already home by the time it got there and the pastor sent it back to America. For the previous five years, ministering to the homeless was the joy of my life, but now, it became a burden. The grace was lifted and I had no joy in serving in this capacity anymore.

I decided to go to California to visit a friend who I met on a singles cruise. Before I went to see her, I purchased a book to give her by Elizabeth Elliot called, <u>Passion and Purity</u>. Little did I know that book was truly meant for me. When I arrived for my visit, Laura had to work every day. I had several hours to read before she came home for the evenings. It was such a beautiful love story between Elizabeth and Jim and of course their days on the mission field. As I read their experiences of love and friendship, I wondered in my heart if that pure love was ever possible. My friend and I spent New Year's Eve, 1993 at Disney World, I remember saying to her, "I wonder what this New Year has in store!"

After I came home from California, there was a note that said, "Joe from Queens called." When I called him back it was exciting to hear his voice, and we made plans to meet on January 27, 1993.

The minute I opened the door to welcome him in, it was like we were never apart. I hadn't seen him in three years, yet, we were so comfortable together. We went to church that day, to dinner and a walk on the beach. When it was time for him to leave, I drove him to the train station. As we sat in the car waiting for the train to come, flashbacks of the book I read about Jim and Elizabeth were just like that.

Jim always visited Elizabeth coming from the train. I felt like we were reenacting the book. My heart was beating so fast, I knew what I wanted to say, so I took his hand and told him if he were to marry someone else or I were to marry someone else that I always wanted to be friends. I was so afraid of losing his friendship. What does that tell you? No way can a man and woman only be friends who love each other that much! The action I took was so out of character for me.

I've had experiences in the past when guys would invite me to dinner, I would say yes, then a little while later I called them back and apologized because I had changed my mind. I had no peace about going on the date, I never wanted to lead anyone on and give the wrong message. With Joe it was different; God was truly placing a love in our hearts for each other.

On the way to visit me, the Lord placed it on Joe's heart that I was going to be his wife. When I told him how I felt, he already knew what I was going to say, because the Lord had already prepared his heart. When he went home he told his mother that I was to be his wife. She was in shock and asked, "How do you know? You haven't even dated her or have seen her in years!"

After he arrived home to Queens from spending the day together, he called me to talk; I found it so easy to talk to him. We made plans to meet again and we were engaged one and a half months later on March 10, 1993. When I told my brother I was getting engaged, he asked, "To who?" I had not been in any relationships, and I was always working on the streets of Manhattan with the homeless. Another day, I sat in the kitchen with my dad, and said to him, "Dad, do you remember Joe from Queens?" and he said, "Yes." I told him, "Get use to him because he's going to be around for a long time." To this day, Joe and my dad are not only son-in-law and father-in-law but great friends as well.

Our engagement was so precious. Not too many couples typically involve their parents and in-laws to be, Joe is different, he did! He proposed with their blessings, and then we went out to a spectacular Japanese restaurant for dinner.

There were so many unique dishes of food to choose from. Some of which were decorated with admirable fruit carvings. The waiters gave us a Japanese umbrella that said, "Congratulations." Outside the venue was a classic Japanese Koi pond with a beautiful red bridge where we took pictures. The scripture that the Lord gave my husband and me when we were engaged was

"Every good gift and perfect gift is from above, coming down from the Father of the heavenly lights, who does not change like shifting shadows" (James 1:17).

Our Engagement

By this time, I was still involved with Hope For The Future. The thought of leaving the ministry to get a job so I could make money didn't give me any peace, so I continued with my duties until the right time arrived. Joe was just out of college and working at a local deli until he found a job in his line of work.

While ministering on the streets, I was approached by an older gentleman. He was one of the senior saints who visited every time we were there. He always told us he didn't need the food but enjoyed the company. He knew I was getting married and handed me what seemed to be a roll of coins. He said quietly, "don't tell anyone," I said, "Thank you" and left. When I went to the van to put it away, I looked at the roll and there were hundred dollar bills rolled up; I counted three thousand dollars! Wow! I promised I wouldn't say a word, I thanked him quietly again and couldn't wait to tell Joe. After work, I drove to Astoria Queens, where Joe was working at a Jewish deli, and ran in with a huge smile on my face and said, "Honey, look what the Lord has done!"

The day I went to the church to ask them to hold the date for our wedding was another miracle. I wanted to be married October 10, the same day as my parents. When I told the secretary I was getting married in October, she said to me, "Pick another month," as that one was filled. I insisted I didn't want another month and asked her to get the calendar. She continued to say the month was full, but when I insisted she reluctantly got the calendar, and to her surprise, there was an opening for October 10. She didn't even know I wanted that particular date.

How good God was to me, to even give me the exact date I wanted. I began looking for a large hall to have our reception. My parents know many people and with Joe's family, we were having three hundred family and friends to celebrate with us. I called so many local places and they were either booked or couldn't accommodate the large crowd. I called the Water Mill in Smithtown and they were booked. A few hours later my mother arrived home and told me she went to the Water Mill and booked our hall. Can you believe it? God was so wonderful to allow me to have all the desires of my heart!

It puts such a smile on my face when I write about all these wonderful miracles.

Everything was gorgeous, just the way I dreamed. Joe moved out to Long Island where I lived and gave up everything he was working so hard for. At one time he wanted to live in the city, but I assured him he was marrying a country girl. Everything was going so nice; God had answered all my prayers and truly given me the desires of my heart. Before we married, I stopped volunteering at Hope For The Future. Believe me, it wasn't easy to do; I truly love being part of that work. But now, my life took a different turn, one that was for my future.

CHAPTER 7

Walking By Faith

For the first five years of our marriage, we lived in my parent's beautiful basement apartment. It was wonderful living with my parents, and it gave Joe and I the ability to work and go to school to complete our degrees.

For many nights, he had dreams of himself walking up and down dark streets crying for the people of the community; where Hispanic and Afro-American people lived. Some of these people were drug addicts. He would wake up feeling sad, crying and wondering where he was and what he was doing there. God was preparing his heart to work in the South Bronx with individuals and families of addiction. A few weeks later, he was hired at the New York Foundling Hospital.

The program he was hired for was to return the children to the parents after they were drug-free. Joe recalls a time when he was called to go into an apartment to review a case to possibly return the child from foster care. It was a dark room with a red light and at the door was a machete. God prepared his heart in the dream so he wouldn't be afraid. He worked there for almost two years commuting every day.

Although we lived in a basement apartment, we decided to begin a family since I was twenty-nine when we married. I had one miscarriage which was so difficult but praise God I conceived again three months later. I was so excited to know a precious baby; my baby was being developed inside of me. What a wonderful miracle!

Joe continued to work at the Foundling Hospital; however, it was getting tiring for him to travel every day such long hours. One day, he was sitting in a conference room, when he began to hear that still gentle voice impress on his heart to ask the man teaching the class for a job. He dismissed the thought and continued listening to the teaching. Again, that small still gentle voice said, "Ask that man for a job." By the third time hearing the voice, he knew he'd better obey.

At the break, he introduced himself and asked the man if he knew of any jobs on Long Island. The man said, "as-a-matter of fact, there is a Spanish speaking drug counselor position open in Hauppauge, Long Island. Here is the phone number, call them and let them know I sent you. "Spanish is Joe's first language." Joe went home and made the phone call; two days later he had the interview. I waited in the car and when I saw my husband walk to the car with a smile on his face, I knew he got the position. Even though he was hired, he still had to take the county test which he did and passed.

Before he left his job at the Foundling Hospital, they were getting ready to celebrate the 125th year of establishment of the New York Foundling Hospital; by the Sisters of Charity at St. Patrick's Cathedral in New York

City 1995. Joe always had a secret desire to take part in a service with Cardinal O'Connor.

One day his boss came to Joe right before he transferred jobs, and said to him, "I can't think of anybody that would be better suited than you to be an acolyte in the service with Cardinal O'Connor to represent us." Joe was elated and was so impressed God gave him the desire of his heart.

Joe as an Acolyte

A few months later, I had a desire to get a degree, so I enrolled at Empire State University and began attending college when I was pregnant with our first child. Everything was going well until my third trimester when I began to swell. My thin face became very full and my legs were so swollen I couldn't see my ankles. Joe and I went for a checkup which was three and a half weeks before I was due. We had just finished Lamaze classes and I wanted so much to deliver naturally.

The minute the nurse took my blood pressure, they wheeled me right over to labor and delivery to perform an emergency C-section. Thank God, Joe was with me. I can still remember myself sitting on the doctor's table shaking uncontrollably. I asked the doctor if I could rest for a while and maybe my blood pressure would drop. He looked at me and said, "Honey, I'm not God, you can have a seizure, a stroke, a coma, or die." I looked at him, and said, "Oh, OK" my husband said at that moment, "What about my wife and baby?" The doctor said, "I don't know!" As they were preparing me for surgery, he went to the chapel and prayed for a safe delivery.

Dr. Vadher, who I love and respect, closed his practice for the remainder of that day and helped Dr. Basile deliver Bethany.

On August 9, 1995, at 8:45 p.m., Bethany Lynn was born. Praise the Lord, all went well and I'm able to write about this story.

She was 5 pounds 13 ounces at birth and I brought her home at 5 pounds 9 ounces. She was so tiny, so perfect and so beautiful. This little bundle of joy would change our life forever. When I first looked at how gorgeous she was, I could not believe she was mine. God gave me another heart's desire.

Bethany Born

When I was a student at Christ For The Nations, I use to pray and ask the Lord to bless me with children from my own womb. After a few months, I went back to school to complete my degree. Bethany would sit in the swing while I wrote my papers or grandma would come downstairs and take her for the day which she loved. Life was so nice.

While working at Joe's new job, he had a desire to complete his Masters in Social Work at Stony Brook University so he enrolled and began taking classes. He finally came to the last part of writing his thesis. My mom would care for Bethany while I worked so he could concentrate. However, my mom would tell me she thought something was wrong with Joe; he was always tired and had no motivation. We always thought it was because he was working full time, completing an internship, and having a new baby, who wouldn't be tired? Even though it was a struggle, he managed to press in and graduate with honors with his Master in Social Work.

Bethany was almost two years old, I had also just graduated from college, getting ready to have another child, and working at Developmental Disability Institute with autistic adults. During this time, my mother was diagnosed with breast cancer, and it was an extremely emotional difficult time. It was one of the worst types a woman could have. She had to have a lumpectomy and go through some radiation treatments; thankfully, she was going to be fine. God was so good to give her wisdom. She was considering taking estrogen and decided not to. If she did, the tumor would have fed on the estrogen and she would not be here today. When I look back on God's provision and His miracles, I can see He truly is Jehovah-Jireh, my Provider, and it encourages me to stand strong.

We were so grateful to have our apartment, but it began to close in on us. I was in the second trimester with our second child and we knew we needed our own home. One day, Joe came home from work and said we're buying a home. I laughed and asked, "With what money?" We were struggling to get an education, we had no money saved. I didn't earn a salary when I worked at Hope For The Future.

Despite our lack of funds, we began turning the TV on and watched the program of the homes for sale. I found an ad for a home in Kings Park, and by faith, we took a drive to see it. Little by little we began to look at more homes until one day,

I received a phone call from Joe while I was working at Developmental Disability Institute. He told me he had put a binder on a home in Hauppauge and to come see it after work. I couldn't believe he had done that without me! However, he went with my mother. It was a ranch with three bedrooms, half an acre of property and on a dead end street, even one of the best school districts for our children. Joe had seen our home once before with the real estate agent and turned it down when he saw the amount of work that had to be done.

The real estate agent called him a second time, so he brought my mother. Sometimes a woman can see things differently and she did. The house was supposed to be ours. Two families before us with a binder on the home fell through, and we were next in line. By faith, the money began to flow in for the down payment. Joe had put some money away without telling me, and our families blessed us so that we had enough for the purchase. What was just a vision became a reality. It was difficult getting the loan since we had such a high back ratio with our college loans, however, the Lord even provided the right person to give us a loan after we were rejected once.

We bought our home in June, and in July, I was in the hospital giving birth to our second child. They admitted me early because they knew my history, and I began to get toxic again. I was not as bad as the first time, but any movement would cause my blood pressure to rise. They gave me my own room, and I had to lie on my left side for five days until the doctor decided to deliver the baby. A nurse came in to monitor me and told me I was having a boy because she had three sons and she carried the same way as I was. To me, it didn't make a difference as long as my baby was healthy.

On July 17, 1998, at 11:02 a.m., my gorgeous daughter, Jessica Marie was born. God blessed us with another girl! As soon as she was born, Joe looked at me and said, "She's gorgeous!" Her tiny little body, with a golden complexion and fuzzy dark hair, was so perfect. She weighed 5 pounds 5 ounces; I brought her home at 5 pounds 2 ounces. I could not believe I was going to be the mother of two precious girls.

Jessica Born

While I was in the hospital, Joe was at our new home painting and preparing it for us. Thankfully we continued to live at my parent's apartment until the house was ready for us to move in. November 1998, when Bethany was three and Jessica was just four months old, we moved into our new home. One year after we moved in our home, I quit my job to stay home and raise our children. Being married, having our children and living in our new home was so much fun and exciting until one day in February 2002, I noticed I had a huge ball in my stomach. My stomach was so large people were asking me if I was pregnant. I really began to feel frightened since I knew I wasn't, and my daughters were so young; Jessica was three and a half and Bethany was six and a half.

I saw Dr. Vadher, and he was concerned I had cancer since the tumors were growing rapidly. I have to admit, I was slightly fearful because, both my parents were diagnosed with cancer a few years before. We immediately made an appointment for surgery and I chose to have my uterus taken out. The total was about seven pounds,

Two tumors were so large they were the size of grapefruits, and I also had several little ones embedded in my uterus.

Before I went to the hospital, I lay next to my daughters in bed telling them how much I loved them; I had no idea what the outcome was going to be. I prayed quietly in my heart and asked the Lord for a positive outcome.

At this time, Joe and I were deciding about having another child, I had to release that desire to the Lord. I know what it's like to have the thoughts plaguing you day and night about dying and leaving my husband to care for my young children. It was a desperate time in our life crying out to God and asking for His mercy for my family. A few days later, we got the results, and Praise God, all went well and it was not cancer!

CHAPTER 8

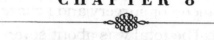

Broken Dreams

Eight months after my surgery, we decided to take the girls to Disney Land in Florida. We enjoyed staying at the Polynesian Hotel and had so much fun going to all the theme parks. We were gone all day and went back to the hotel in the evening. I just wanted to rest a little, and then go back to the parks again, but Joe was tired and needed to relax. I couldn't understand why he wanted to stay in the hotel room and rest because we were on vacation and needed to experience everything.

When we came home, he decided to go to the doctors to have blood work done. Everything was fine, except his liver enzymes were slightly elevated. The doctor asked if he was taking any Tylenol and Joe told him he did because he injured his back while doing yard work. The doctor explained not to worry about it because Tylenol could raise the levels. We continued our life as normal; however, Joe was still not feeling well. He was always extremely tired and had no energy. For him, that was out of character because he's always on the go.

When he went to work one day at the health clinic, he asked the phlebotomist to draw his blood to check his labs for everything. When the phlebotomist got the results a few days later, she said to him, "I have something serious to tell you, do you want the doctor to tell you or me?" He allowed the phlebotomist to tell him the results, and she said, "You have hepatitis C." He was somewhat in shock, thinking it was a mistake, but then realized it was true. When he came home, he sat down with me to break the news. It was a very deep dark lonely place for us to be. A few months ago we were having such a great time at Disney Land with the girls and celebrated ten years of marriage, and now, a few weeks after, we were facing the biggest challenge of our life.

We made an appointment in April 2003, for Joe to have a liver biopsy and discovered, his liver was in stage three-four which means the liver has moderate to severe fibrosis which is scaring and inflammation; heading toward cirrhosis of the liver.

Right before this took place, my husband and I were reading the book of Job. We were at the part when Satan answered the Lord and told Him he was roaming the earth and going back and forth in it. Isn't it amazing how the Lord said to Satan, "Have you considered my servant Job?" Satan replied, "Have you not put a hedge around him and his household and everything he has? You have blessed the work of his hands so that his flocks and herds are spread throughout the land. Stretch out your hand and strike everything he has, and he will surely curse you to your face." It almost reminded me of myself, I've had people tell me before that I'm spoiled and that

God always gives me what I want. I usually laugh and say, "Spoiled? No! Blessed? Yes!"

I felt as though Satan approached God and there was a battle going on in Heaven. I can just picture God conversing with Satan, "What about my servants Joe and Debbie?" Everything I've ever hoped for, our plans for the future, our dreams, I felt as though they were crushed. No one had any answers, my mind rushed to despair, and thoughts that were filled with death and destruction. It's amazing what happened to me when I received such news.

My first reaction was sobering; a thought process began to happen. Okay, what does this mean? How can he be treated? What if there is no treatment? On and on my mind began to spin. I was in shock about what we just heard, heartbroken and desperate. Something else began to happen within the next couple of days, almost disbelief, and denial of what I heard. "It can't be, we haven't even accomplished what we know You want us to do." Another process began to happen and that is, I began to become disillusioned; "it's not fair!" I felt like my trust was broken like God had abandoned me. I began to cry out to the Lord, "I waited patiently for my husband; I was twenty-nine when we married, we're so happy and now You're going to take him?" These emotions were all the process of grieving.

Lesson #1 Identify Your Grief: If you are going through any illness or tragedy in your life, grief must be identified. Don't bury it deep in your heart, it will get worse. You may need to go to counseling to identify every area in which you feel broken. Don't walk in denial, acknowledge and confront it.

Grief happens to all of us when we're given shocking and unbelievable news. I once heard it said, "Grief denied is a grief unhealed." We all will face some sort of grief while we're traveling on life's road. All the emotions of shock, pain, disbelief, unfairness, loneliness, depression, anxiety, abandonment and fear will strike you at one time in your life because we are all a part of this world. The road to recovery will not be easy.

A. **The Good News Is, Jesus Bore Our Griefs and Sorrows:** Jesus himself was a man of sorrows and familiar with suffering. He can heal your broken heart and restore your joy and peace because He carried your sorrows when He went to the cross. By reminding myself of these truths, I began to feel peace.

When you think of the word "cross" what comes to mind? A person carrying a cross in first century Palestine was about to be executed. Anxiety comes to my mind; anguish, suffering, loneliness, pain, hardship, blood, death. I'm sure you can think of other characteristics. When I said before that, "Jesus bore our sins and sickness on the cross," He became sin for us. He made Atonement for our sins. To atone means to take away completely. He completely took away our sin and "by His stripes we are healed." He made a covenant with us. He took all those feelings we go through and replaced them with the opposite. Anxiety was placed with peace. Jesus is the Prince of Peace. *"You will keep him in perfect peace, whose mind is stayed on You because he trusts in You"* *(Isaiah 26:3).*

Notice There is a condition to having peace? We have to **keep our mind focused on Jesus,** the Messiah so we may receive His peace. To keep our mind focused on Jesus means to, read our Bible, to pray, listen to Godly worship music, to fill yourself with Him and above all, trust Him through your trial. By doing this, when we carry our cross we will keep our thoughts upon Jesus.

The Bible tells us to *"pick up our cross and follow Him."* He does not tell us to walk away, throw it away or to burn it, He clearly says, *"Pick up your cross"* and do what? *"Follow me."* Many people don't want to pick up their cross, but, then he says to them all, *"If anyone would come after Me, he must deny himself and take up his cross daily and follow Me. For whoever wants to save his life will lose it, but whoever loses his life for My sake will save it"* *(Luke 9:23-24).*

Honestly, I didn't want this cross in my life, I didn't want to pick it up, however, I had no choice and neither did my family. Instead of becoming angry, like many people do, we picked up our cross and walked by faith.

It sounds difficult, not many people want to deny themselves, but look what happens when you are obedient. Your anguish will turn to joy, your anxiety will turn to peace, and fear will turn to love. He exchanged the anguish for joy,

"He endured the cross for the joy that was set before him." He did not look back but He pressed on, He could have gotten off the cross, He's God. He could have struck them all dead, but His love for us held Him there and He looked beyond what was happening. He kept his eyes focused on the joy that was set before him for humankind. He was soon to be given dominion over death to destroy the works of the devil. He would soon be seated with God the Father and ruling and reigning with Him.

Read the book of Hebrews. Remember, one of our precious promises is that" *God raised us up with Christ and seated us with Him in the heavenly realms Christ Jesus" (Ephesians 2:6).*

B. **The Joy Of The Lord Is Your Strength:** I knew I needed my strength to endure the battle before me. When you spend time with the Lord you will be filled with joy because "In His presence there is fullness of joy." His desire is to fill you with joy.

When you're tired mentally, emotionally, and spiritually the battle seems so much harder and blown out of proportion. This is why it is so extremely important to get the proper rest so you will be alert to be able to fight the good fight of faith. He exchanged the feelings of loneliness with a relationship. That is why He created you; for fellowship.

C. Jesus Can Identify With Loneliness: Jesus can identify with the loneliness you may be going through. When He hung on the cross enduring the suffering and shame He cried out, "Father, why have You forsaken Me?" Have you ever felt forsaken? I have felt forsaken, but

D. Don't Believe Those Lies: I know the enemy wants to cripple you so you're left with no power and no covering from the Lord who loves you the most and gave His life for you. What Jesus did despite His feelings was; He cried to His Father "Forgive them for they know not what they are doing."
Learn to forgive and you will be healed.

E. Cry Out In Submission: When you cry out with prayers and petitions as long as you do it with reverence and a submissive heart, God Almighty hears you.

Jesus was born to suffer and die for you and for me. When He knew He was going to the cross, He cried out, "Lord let this cup pass from me." He knows what it's like to suffer and cry out. The Bible states, *"During the days of Jesus' life on earth, he offered up prayers and petitions with loud cries and tears to the one who could save him from death, and he was heard because of his reverent submission" (Hebrew 5:11).* Read this again until it becomes real in your heart. Jesus was crying out to God the Father to deliver him from this great pain. However, God had an ultimate plan and purpose; Jesus had to be obedient even to death. God's great plan was for Him to shed His blood for us so that we might live and be forgiven and healed. How many times do we cry out to God to deliver us?

We Must Ask God What His Plan and Purpose Is.
Jesus cried aloud and yielded himself and His own will to God the Father's. When He cried out, He also said, "Nevertheless, not my will but thine be done." God the Father then sent Jesus, God the Son, ministering angels to fill Him with the ability, which is the grace to be able to go through the task that was set before Him.

Praise the Lord for His obedience and for the outcome, He rose again and broke the powers of death, and because He lives we can live too! We can have the assurance that, *"Even though we die, yet will we live" (John 11:25).*

How did Jesus learn obedience? It was through the things He suffered! Wow! Can you imagine the King of Glory had to learn obedience by the things He suffered? (Hebrews 5:8) It's very difficult to comprehend that Jesus had to learn obedience, but what a wonderful example we have to follow.

Because Jesus suffered He can identify with the suffering you and I may be going through. If we *"humble ourselves in the sight of the Lord, He will lift you up"* (James 4:10).

CHAPTER 9

❧

What is Hepatitis C?

Before I continue with my story, I would like to discuss what hepatitis C is. Hepatitis was first identified in 1989. Before this, it was called Non A or Non-B hepatitis. There are millions of people who have it throughout the world. Although in 2003, very seldom did you hear about this disease.

There are several forms of hepatitis including A, B and so forth. I'm going to discuss hepatitis C. This virus is transmitted through blood to blood contact. Could be sex, infected needle drug use or years ago, they gave people immunizations with the same needle that promoted the hepatitis virus. Also, same needle usage when getting a tattoo. Many people were also infected through tainted blood during blood transfusions. I also met a dental hygienist who contracted this disease many years ago when gloves were not worn. Unfortunately, blood tests to detect the hepatitis C virus were not available before 1990. For that reason, anyone who had a transfusion or surgery before then is at a higher risk to contract this disease. Believe it or not, hepatitis C is one of the fastest-growing diseases in America, China, and Australia.

Hepatitis C lays dormant in your body for about twenty-five years before you realize you have it and it could be too late. Because the virus has no side effects for many years, most people don't realize they have it. This is why the disease is called the "silent killer," In the coming years; we can expect many thousands of people to develop HCV (Hepatitis C Virus) related cirrhosis, which many will need liver transplants.

Doctors do not check for hepatitis. It is usually found out by accident. My husband had three blood transfusions when he was in a car accident in the early eighties. At this time, they were taking the blood from the homeless population due to the blood shortage. (Yes, I had to lay my feelings down on that one too, "Lord that's not fair! I worked and served You on the streets with the homeless for years and the very thing I served You with is going to destroy my husband's life and mine?" I definitely had to lay that one at the foot of the cross and leave it there).

Understanding Your Liver

Your liver is located in your upper right part of your abdomen under your rib cage. Next to your skin, it is the largest organ in your body. Your liver is so important and has many functions, let me share some with you.

*Storing energy in the form of sugar
*Storing vitamins, iron, and other minerals
*Making protein, including blood clotting factors
*Process worn out blood cells

*Makes bile that helps digest food
*Cleans the blood by breaking down medicines and toxins such as alcohol.
*Regenerates its own damaged tissue
*Maintains hormone balance
*Helps in absorption of fat-soluble vitamins including A,D,E,K
*Helps the body resist infection by producing immune factors and removing bacteria from the blood. [1]

The liver does so much that I never knew about, and finding out my husband has this disease answers many questions. Now we know why he always felt tired.

One symptom of a sluggish liver is fatigue. To overcome chronic fatigue syndrome we must take the load off the overworked immune system by cleansing the liver. Cleansing the liver is extremely important, even if you don't have liver disease.

It's important to do this to keep healthy. Many people eat unhealthily and can get a fatty liver, which can develop cirrhosis.

"A common symptom of an overworked or toxic liver is excessive body heat."

I found this to be most interesting because my husband has always been hot. His body temperature was always at least ten degrees higher than mine. If you ever have symptoms of any kind, never ignore them and

[1] Center for Liver Disease & Transplantation New York Presbyterian Hospital

ask questions. The Bible does say, "My people perish for lack of wisdom."

Two years ago when Joe had his yearly physical his liver enzymes were elevated. The doctors didn't seem to be alarmed so neither were we. We didn't even know what the word enzyme meant and that it was serious. I'll take a minute to explain what it is. I have learned so much due to my husband having his blood drawn frequently.

"The reasons why all or some of these liver enzymes become elevated in cases of liver disease is that they are normally contained inside the liver cells (hepatocytes). When the enzymes leak into the bloodstream the liver cells are inflamed.

This is especially true of ALT, which exists mostly in liver cells and has more specificity for monitoring liver inflammation than AST does. The AST and ALT blood tests help to measure liver enzymes which are used to detect liver damage.

AST (Aspartate aminotransferase) can also be elevated in liver, heart and muscle disease. Normal range is 5-54U/L. ALT-(Alaine aminotransferase) is more specific for liver damage. Normal range is 9/60 U/L."[2]

[2] Healing Hepatitis C with Modern Chinese Medicine
Qingcai Zhang, M.D. Sino-Med Institute, New York, copyright: 2000, p.32

Nutrition

It is very important to have a healthy liver because it detoxifies everything and has so many functions to perform. After my husband was diagnosed with this disease we decided to cleanse our liver. Everything we eat, breath and all the toxins we absorb through our skin like cleaning chemicals are filtered through the liver. After hearing the news of my husband's liver disease we wanted to make his liver as healthy as possible. I also decided to cleanse my liver along with Joe; it can never hurt, only help.

The symptoms of a toxic or sick liver are abdominal bleeding, sugar cravings, excessive body heat, high blood pressure, overweight, poor digestion, and much more. I decided my whole way of cooking had to change; I wanted to see my husband healed. We began to eat more fruits and vegetables, I juiced for us every day and we drank water and lemon every morning. This is very good to cleanse your liver.

Just to give you an idea, every morning have an eight-ounce glass of water and lemon, a few minutes later drink a fresh glass of carrot, parsley, celery, and beet juice. Beet is what cleanses the blood. For breakfast have oatmeal or whole grain cereal with almond or rice or coconut milk. Cut out all sugar, coffee, anything with caffeine, white flour products, dairy, peanut & peanut butter, all refined and processed foods which means all cold cuts. For lunch have a whole grain sandwich with avocado, tomatoes lettuce, or any kind of soup, a salad with chicken, turkey, sardines or tuna.

Dinner have steamed or raw veggies, a sweet potato, a hearty soup, fresh fish. Cut out all red meat which may be hard for you, so if you have to have it, have it once a week and antibiotic free. Red meat is harder to digest. Stop all dairy products. Eat liver friendly foods which would be Artichokes, Asparagus, Avocados, Beets, Broccoli, Brussel Sprouts, Cabbage, Carrots, Cauliflower, Celery, Chicory, Garlic, Leeks, and Onions, Radishes.

Stay away from foods that have too much iron, such as liver, beef, iron-fortified cereals, and spinach. Too much iron can be toxic to the liver. Also, try not to eat heavy rich foods with cream and cheese. Eat brown rice, pasta, beans, raw fruits, and veggies. Try not to over eat for this is no good for digestion. You want to stay away from all processed foods and eat only natural things. The idea is you want to put less strain on the liver since everything is filtered through it. It may be difficult, but if you want to live you will do anything. There have been hundreds and even thousands of people changing their diets and totally getting rid of their illness.

"Faith without Works is Dead" (James 2:17).

CHAPTER 10

❈

Testing of Your Faith

One day I was reading my Bible and I came across this scripture. "Consider it pure joy my brethren, whenever you face trials of many kinds because you know that the **TESTING** *of your faith develops perseverance. Perseverance must finish its work so that you may be mature and complete" (James 1: 2-4).*

After I quoted that scripture found in James, I took a few days to really ponder on that scripture. "Consider it joy when you go through trials" Huh? That doesn't seem fair! How can I consider it joy when our life has been shattered by this devastating news? It seemed as though we were thrown in a deep, dark, pit and we were never going to escape.

Before we went to the doctor to begin treatment, we took a few days to ask God what He was doing in our lives, and also to meditate on God's Word. We traveled to see a doctor in Manhattan that came recommended. Joe and I were brought in a room to discuss treatment with Interferon and Ribavirin. The doctor explained he wanted to treat Joe aggressively and explained all the negative side effects including depression and suicidal thoughts.

It seemed as though the side effects were worse than the disease. I want to explain that there are different strains of hepatitis C, he has genotype 1a.

After seeing the doctor and hearing the medical report, we felt like we really didn't have any other alternatives, so Joe began taking this medication. It was very scary watching him inject some foreign medication into his body. This drug is a form of chemotherapy; it's breaking down his immune system. Every time we go to the doctors, it's as if they pronounce a death sentence over him; "Cirrhosis of the liver? We'll have to perform radical treatment."

Remember, the year was 2003 and the only type of medication for this illness was Interferon and Ribavirin. After Joe took the medication twice, he had to stop treatment. He had severe side effects, worse than the doctors anticipated. If he continued using the medication, it could have killed him. All that came out of my mouth, while watching him in pain was, "Jesus help!"

My Journal: Today is June 3, 2003. It's been two months since my husband's diagnosis, and I'm crying out to the Lord, "Please help! Jesus, You promised, You're as close to the mention of Your name. Jesus, have mercy on Your child. Lord, if my daughter is sick I'll do everything I can to relieve her pain. Lord, Joe is Your child, please Lord, relieve him of his pain. He's in so much pain, it's unbearable. My heart is breaking and I'm screaming out to You. He's been given only two years to live!"

Several years ago I received a prophetic word not to look with the eyes of the flesh, but to look with the eyes of the Spirit. It's at those times, in your life, at the darkest hour, when you have to see with the eyes of the Spirit. In other words using the faith that comes with trusting God, "Lord, I am going to call those things that are not as though they are." I see healing upon my husband in Jesus' Mighty Name. Every time I imagined my husband's funeral, I quickly changed my thoughts and imagined him in a suit preaching the Word of God. I want to tell you and proclaim the victory that when no one had the answer, Jesus did. His Word is filled with promises that we need to meditate upon.

A few days after taking the medication the side effects began to appear. His skin literally peeled off his body. Every time he got up from where he was sitting or lying, there were large piles of ashes from his skin. He looked as though he belonged in a burn unit in a hospital. His skin was on fire day and night, and when we went to the doctor they said, "Sorry, there's nothing we can do." Going to the emergency room was just a waste of time. They didn't even know what the medication was for, I had to tell them. There were days we didn't know what to do, there were no answers! I bought an aloe plant and rubbed it all over his skin, he also took baths to cool his high fever, and sometimes it went as high as one hundred and four to one hundred and five.

How do we consider it pure joy when we see the one we love so weak that he can't lift his head off the pillow? When he finally did lift his head off the pillow to try to get up, he was in so much pain he just shook uncontrollably. In my own flesh, I wanted to scream and say to James the author of this chapter, "You've got to be kidding! This is no joke; it's more like a frightening nightmare."

Speaking By Faith

In my next few pages, I will describe how I am speaking the Word in prayer for my husband's healing. "Jesus, we trust You *"And we know that in all things God works for the good of those who love him, who have been called according to his purpose"* (Romans 8:28).

I don't see him physically well yet, but I believe I will. I refuse to watch my husband deteriorate before my eyes and die. It's hard not to believe the flesh, he's lost thirty pounds, he's weak and tired, his skin color is gray, he's bleeding abdominally, he has cramps that are so severe he can't get out of bed, his urine is extremely dark, his vision is beginning to go blurry, his skin is red hot and is burning day in and day out. He has fevers of one hundred and four to one hundred and five; his gorgeous thick dark hair is beginning to thin, and he lost a chunk of it the other day. NO! I will not look at his body; my God, You promised, that by "Your stripes we are healed!" "I know the answer is in You, Lord; I will continue to praise Your name." When I fill myself with praise and sing unto the Lord, He is faithful to fill me with joy. Sing unto the Lord a new song. He will lift you up!

In the natural, he had to stop the medication, there's no conventional treatment for him; everything failed! The doctors can only say, "I'm sorry, maybe in another five years, we'll come out with a new medication." Five years? They said he'll only have two years if he's not treated. My head is overwhelmed, my heart is fading. I laid my elbows on the kitchen table sobbing and begging God to heal my husband from this debilitating disease and side effects. All of a sudden it hit me, I felt as though I was begging God like a dog begs for food. You don't need to beg God.

Lesson #2 Approach The Throne Of God: We need to approach the throne of God with confidence, and boldness knowing that He hears our prayers and is ready and willing to help in time of need. *"My son, pay attention to what I say; listen closely to My words. Do not let them out of your sight, keep them within your heart, for they are life to those who find them and health (medicine) to a man's whole body" (Proverbs 4:20-23).*

When I read this Scripture I can hear a father talking to his child, "Pay attention to what I say" How many times can you hear yourself saying that to your child? Remember your parents saying that to you? "It's extremely important, again I will tell you, PAY ATTENTION! Listen closely to My words. Never let them out of your sight, keep them so close to you they are in your heart. Why am I telling you this with such urgency, my child? Because I love you.

If you will listen carefully and do what I say you will find life and health, even for your whole body." The word *"health"* in this verse translated to the original Greek means *"medicine."* Keep His Word in your heart and speaking out of your mouth because it is medicine. The scripture will heal you just as medicine does without all the negative side effects.

I repeated every day, Lord, You promised *"With long life will I satisfy him and show him my salvation" (Psalm 91:16)*. Remember what the word salvation means, to "protect, heal, deliver." "With long life, will You satisfy Joe and show him Your salvation." I repeated day after day, *"I (Joe) will not die but live and will proclaim what the Lord has done" (Psalm 118:17)*. Rebuke that filthy spirit of death in the Name of Jesus.

A. Walk By Faith: I began to walk around the house and put scriptures on my walls. When he opened his bedroom closet he saw, *"I will extol (bless) the Lord at all times, His praise will always be on my lips" (Psalm 34:1)*. "I will bless Thee oh Lord, with a heart of thanksgiving I will bless Thee oh Lord." Once you read these words, it will become a song in your heart and your mouth will continue to speak it; there is power in what you speak. With your tongue, you can speak life and curses.

B. Cry Out To The Lord Because He Hears You: Have you ever been given a death sentence? Rebuke it in the Name of Jesus! Cry out to the Lord because He

77

hears you. I began to shout out *"Lord, my husband will not die, but live and will proclaim what the Lord has done"* (Psalm 118:17).

What I was doing was confessing by faith. My thoughts were, "Lord, You've put me through great trials before, but this one Lord, WOW! My faith can really be shaken. I have two young daughters who love their daddy. Bethany is only seven and a half and Jessica is only four and a half years old. "Oh Jesus, will I be a single mother?

What about all our dreams and visions You promised?" "With long life will I satisfy him and show him my salvation." As you can see, I repeated these two scriptures several times throughout the day. I commanded my spirit to rise up and take hold of all God's promises.

C. Speak The Word: *"So is My Word that goes out from my mouth; It will not return to me empty, but will accomplish what I desire and achieve the purpose for which I sent it"* (Isaiah 55:11). As my husband was sick, I pleaded the blood over him constantly. You may ask why I was doing this. As I stated before, there is power in the Blood of Jesus. I simply say, "Jesus, cover Joe with Your precious Blood."

Don't allow the devil any room, he loves to torment and bring defeat. Learn to "take every thought captive and make it obedient to Christ Jesus." What do I mean by that? Begin to quote the scripture back to the Lord; His Word is filled with promises and power. His Word is alive.

"Then they cried to the Lord in their trouble, and He saved them from their distress. He sent His word and healed them; He rescued them from the grave" (Psalm 107:19-20).

I began to speak the Word back to Jesus. Lord, You promised that Joe is a "new creation, old things are passed away behold all things are new." Lord, You made his spirit new, his emotions new, now Lord, make his body new. Make it personal by putting your name in it. You also promised that *"We are your workmanship created in you that you have good works for us to do that has been prepared in advance"* (Ephesians 2:10).

Thank-You Jesus; *"You are a good God and you are a rewarder of those who diligently seek you"* (Hebrews 11:6). "Jesus, my husband has sought You, Oh Lord answer his call." Your promise says, *"Surely the arm of the Lord is not too short to save, nor his ear too dull to hear"* (Isaiah 59:1). *"He fulfills the desires of those who fear him; He hears their cry and saves them, the Lord watches all who love him"* (Psalm 145:19). Lord, you also promised *"If you honor your father and mother, it may go well with you and that you may enjoy long life on the earth"* (Ephesians 6:3). Joe has honored his parents, even with our engagement.

D. Speak To Your Soul: *"Oh why be downcast oh my soul put your trust in God the maker of heaven and earth"* (Psalm 43:5). Sing and praise the Lord. He inhabits the praises of his people. I thought to myself, everything I've ever been taught has to be real, God, show Yourself to us. Do you think God showed up? I was wishing He would appear, did He? No! I was desperate, crying my heart out at times, "God, where are You? Lord, Joe, the one You love needs You. Did He make an appearance? Not physically, but He came through people.

Family and friends began to pray. People began to come to our house for a prayer meeting; which my cousins Danny and Jessie started. God met us in mighty ways. Through songs, prophecy, prayer and encouragement. He brought comfort reassuring us of His love. Telling us with God all things are possible.

He began to bring peace and comfort in ways that only He can bring. He spoke to us by saying, "I love you, honor Me and lift Me up from the earth." "My child, I am God and there is nothing impossible with Me, I am God, I will heal you, I have healed you, I love you, Joe. You've walked with Me, I remember all those things, I will take care of you, honor Me, look upon Me, worship Me."

The very thing I prayed about the Lord heard. When I was at the table crying, I was reminding Him, telling the Lord, Joe? Not Joe, he loves You. How the Lord even called him by name that was so beautiful. When the doctors gave us no hope and when the sickness from this medication was lasting for months, the Lord brought comfort to us, Thank-You Mighty God.

In one of the prayer meetings there was some confusion, but after singing and bringing in the presence of the Lord, it was evident what was happening. When we prayed for Joe he saw a bright light going thru his body, he felt the Holy Spirit touch him. It was also a time for me to wail and weep before the Lord, with the support of family and friends. When they prayed for me, it was as though the spirit inside of me was deeply groaning with great travail and great pain and sorrow.

This cry came from the inner part of my belly, it was so intense, nothing I ever encountered before. I remember crying out saying, "No Lord, not my girls" (meaning I didn't want them to be fatherless). I also told the Lord, "I'll do whatever You want me to do and I'll go where ever You want me to go, just heal Joe."

E. Get Prayer: Another day I called our pastors for prayer: All the pastors prayed with great intensity and authority. The Lord also gave us a word at the meeting. He confirmed in our hearts that He heard our cries and that He would heal my husband. As we left the prayer meeting our hearts were so overjoyed with gladness. We truly went from feeling downhearted to being encouraged and strengthened for the next move. In the meantime, even though God was filling us spiritually, we still had to deal with the pain and sickness my husband was going through.

It was so sad to see him go through times of depression. I came home from work one day to find him sitting on the front porch with tears running down his cheeks. He had to come home from being at Walmart because he felt so sick. He said to me, "If I have to live like this, with no quality of life and not to be able to play with our girls I don't want to live." We talked about it, and God gave him the strength to carry on. By now, he had to stop the medication and was still fighting through all the side effects. *"The eyes of the Lord are on the righteous and His ears are attentive to their cry"* (Psalm 34:15).

It's amazing to see the things that are being birthed in our lives after this diagnosis of my husband's illness. First, I will no longer refer to it as a trial of adversity, but as being in the will of God. My attitude is changing. Our attitude is a very powerful influence. My attitude is allowing me to live a life of surrender to God's will in my life. It is so important to have a good attitude, because if you don't, poor attitude will discourage you, destroy you, and cause you to totally give up on life.

Second, our precious prayer meeting began in our home with family and friends, even if it's for a season. The amazing part about this prayer meeting is before Joe and I were married, God gave me a dream that our home would be a home where people came for healing. You heard my prayer I prayed when I was single.

The third thing that has taken place is this book that the Lord placed on my heart to write. The Lord gave me the desire to write a book many years ago and I never knew what it was going to be about. I thought, Lord, I never went through anything. I've had a wonderful life, what could I ever write about? Be careful what you ask!

Question: What's being birthed in your life during your emotional transition?

_____

_____

_____

Question: How are you handling your present situation? Is God in control or are you?

_____

_____

_____

Ponder: God loves you so much that He promises to never leave you or forsake you.

CHAPTER 11

Spiritual Warfare

It was shocking, difficult, and a struggle to stand strong when I first heard about my husband's medical condition; everything I've been taught since I was a child began to play over and over in my mind. In one ear, I could hear all the stories of Jesus healing people, and in the other ear, I heard defeat. My mind and emotions were trying to waver from the truth that I knew. I had to either press in or I was going to give in and let my emotions dictate my life and get the best of my family and me. I began to remember everything I was taught at Bible school on "Spiritual Warfare" remember, that was also another favorite topic of mine.

One thing I did know, I had to rise up and take hold of my thoughts. We were in another battle. I didn't have time to have a pity party for myself or my family, I had to rise up and fight with the weapons God had provided.

Lesson #3 Gods' Weapons: In your everyday battle of life and hardships we must put on the full armor of God to overcome our weaknesses such as depression, fear, anxiety, worry, and hopelessness. Don't concern yourself, the Lord said, "The battle is Mine." You may think the battle is against your spouse, sibling, neighbor, employee or even illness. The Bible says, *"For our struggle is not against flesh and blood, but against the rulers, against the authorities, against the powers of this dark world and against the spiritual forces of evil in the heavenly realms" (Ephesians 6:12).*

Yes, it is spiritual warfare! What does the Bible say? Sit back, relax and go to sleep, become lazy and retreat to an emotional basket case? No, the Bible says, *"Therefore put on the full armor of God, so that when the day of evil comes, you may be able to stand, and after you have done everything to stand" (Ephesians 6:13).*

A. Dig Your Feet In A Little Deeper and Stand Firm: Don't allow yourself to get blown over and to be taken by the wind or to get consumed in the fire, stand your ground and buckle up!

B. Make Sure Your Roots Are Dug Deep In The Word of God: If they are not, that is when you will want to quit the fight.

Weapon 1 - Belt Of Truth: Fit your belt of truth tightly around your waist and stand firm so when testing's come you won't be uprooted from what you believe. You won't be tossed in the wind of doubt and unbelief, but you will **Stand Strong in Faith and Trust.** Remember, you have the truth, don't allow yourself to listen to the lies of hopelessness. *"Stand firm then with the belt of truth buckled around your waist" (Ephesians 6:14).*

Vision: A picture that comes to my mind is a small tree that has just been planted. When you want the tree to grow straight and firm in the ground you place an anchor next to it, and harness a strong rope around the tree. When the winds come it won't get knocked out of balance or become uprooted. It will stand strong and grow straight until all the roots begin to take root. When the roots are deep in the ground the tree will never get knocked over. Your roots should be dug deep in the Word of God and Jesus Christ the Rock of your salvation; this comes by reading and meditating on His Word.

A. **Wrap Your Mind On Christ:** Especially now, I had to remember that I was stronger than any problem or disappointment life brought. My roots, which are my belief system, were wrapped on Christ, the Messiah, the Solid Rock. I knew I had to press in and fight with everything I have learned and put it into practice or I was going to give up and be depressed.

**Unless You Go through Difficulties,
You'll Never Know How Deep Your Roots Really Are.**

Have you ever noticed an oak tree during a storm? In most cases the oak tree will bend its branches; sometimes a branch will break off, the leaves may be blown all around. But if the oak tree has its roots deep in the ground, even though it may bend and break after the storm it's standing upright. Only those trees that are not grounded will get blown over. Determine to be like that oak tree, strong and firm.

You may be swayed from left to right, but after the wind is gone, you're standing upright looking to the "Son."

Question: Are your roots wrapped around the Word of God so that you can stand through the storm?

God's desire is that you will come into a place of trusting Him while in your flames; so that together you and I may be equipped to fight against the enemy and all of his schemes.

Weapon 2 - Breast Plate: After the belt of truth is on, put the Breastplate of Righteousness in place. God sees us standing before Him cleansed because of His blood. No human being is righteous; we have all sinned and fallen short of God's glory. if we have faith in Jesus, we are freed from the power of sin, given new life, and returned to a right relationship with God. He sees us, not as we are but cleansed by the Blood of Jesus, *"The battle has been won by the blood and by the word of your testimony" (Revelations 12:11).*

How many of you have a testimony? I know you all do; you can see His mercy toward you every day. He has been faithful to take you out and clothe you with righteousness and adopt you as His own children. He does not call you slaves, but sons and daughters, joint heirs with Him. *"We are a chosen generation, a royal priesthood, a holy nation" (1 Peter 2:9).*

This reveals to us that we are accepted and clothed with the robe of righteousness. Meaning we are to put off the old man and his ways; negative thinking, negative actions, bad attitudes . . ., and we are to put on the new man righteous thinking, actions. . .,which is created in righteousness (Ephesians 4:24).

A. **Don't Be Defeated:** Don't look at yourself as defeated, but as right standing with God. When you are right standing with God, everything is made right. He will bring to order everything that seems to be in disorder. **Notice how the breastplate is placed on your chest to protect your heart?** Your heart is the inner core of a human, it is what speaks, your *heart is the reflection of a man (Proverbs 27:19).*

B. **Don't Think Defeat, Think Victory:** There is victory in Jesus! Your thoughts are what can defeat you. I don't know if this happens to you, but I can be driving in my car, and my thoughts can get away with me, and before I know it tears are rolling down my cheeks. When this happens I have to change my thinking, and then God helps me to put a smile on my face to continue the day with strength and confidence.

C. **Keep Your Thoughts On God:** Keep your thoughts on God and His Word so that you can walk in victory and perfect peace. To experience God's peace and freedom from anxiety you have to fix your mind on those things that are true, right and pure.

If you do these things, "The God of peace will be with you." If you choose not to keep your mind fixed on Christ then the consequence is God's peace is lost and your heart is not guarded. Remember, guard your heart and keep it with all diligence.

Weapon 3 - Shoes Of Peace: Fit your feet with the readiness that comes from the Gospel of Peace *"The Lord gives strength to his people; the Lord blesses his people with peace" (Psalm 29:11)*. Jesus will give you peace in the midst of uncertain circumstances. In return, you can go forth and bring the comfort of peace to others that God bestowed on you.

Weapon 4 - Shield Of Faith: In addition, above all *"take up the Shield of Faith, with which you can extinguish all the flaming arrows of the evil one" (Ephesians 6:16)*. *"Every word of God is pure; He is a shield to those who put their trust in Him" (Proverbs 30:5)*. Notice how He is a shield to those that trust Him? Once you trust Him, you can lift up the shield of faith knowing the shield will extinguish all the lies that will be thrown at you. "You're no good, you're a failure, you'll never amount to anything, you'll never complete the call of God on your life, and you're going to die."

Picture how small the mustard seed is, it's as tiny as a pinhead. The Bible clearly says if you have faith as tiny as a mustard seed you can say to this mountain be removed and it will be gone. The mustard seed is very small and sometimes I feel like my faith is as small as that. This is where I say, "Lord, I believe but help my unbelief." The mustard seed is known to grow into the largest tree. A small amount of faith will do large things. Speaking by faith even if you think it's small will grow large and defeat the enemy, read (Mark 4:30-32).

What mountain do you have in your life? It could be anything that is preventing you from what God intends you to be. It is impossible to please God without faith; the whole Christian life is a faith walk. What is faith? Hoping for those things we do not yet have, believing in the promises that God has given to you, even when you don't see them. "Faith is never a denial of reality. It is a belief in a greater reality; God!"

Weapon 5 - Helmet Of Salvation: God also wants us to put on the helmet of Salvation knowing what Jesus did for you at the cross; He died on the cross for your salvation. He came to seek and to save the lost. He came to bring eternal life which is a free gift, salvation. My husband always reminds me that salvation is free, but following Jesus will cost you everything. In other words strive to live a holy life, He wants all of you, everything you think, everything you do, do it for His glory and not your own and when you go wrong the Blood of Christ removes all sin.

A. Action Words: Notice, there are two action words you must do to be saved? First, you have to **confess** the

Word with your mouth; second, You have to believe with your heart that what you say is true. Read that Scripture again and take a moment to think about it. Notice one of the weapons God gave us is the helmet of salvation? He gives us a helmet to protect our mind. What we confess will tell what state of mind we are in.

B. **Confess The Promises Of God:** Confess the promises of God and allow a transformation to take place. Confession is what we think and who we are. It is a very powerful tool God gave us. Confess with your mouth, "Thank You, Jesus, I am healed." "Thank You, Jesus, You love me." "Thank You I am saved and a child of the most High and want You only the best for me."

Weapon 6 - Sword Of The Spirit:

A. **Speak The Promises Of God:** Thank God for the Word, the Sword of the Spirit. Don't be overtaken by those lies, allow faith to come out of your mouth like a sword. "You liar, I am the righteousness of God in Jesus Christ, I am the head and not the tail. He sees me cleansed by His blood. *"I can do everything through Him who gives me strength" (Philippians 4:13).*

B. **Replace The Lies:** Replace those lies with His Word, the Truth. Step out of your natural thinking and speak the supernatural, replacing those thoughts with the truth, the weapon God gave you to counteract the attack.

I'm imagining you holding your shield in front of you and every negative word that is spoken is bouncing off and does not penetrate to your heart. By doing this you are trusting God and He will extinguish all the lies of the enemy. *"We demolish arguments and every pretension that set itself up against the knowledge of God, and we take every thought captive and make it obedient to Christ Jesus" (2 Corinthians 10:5).*

Our thoughts are what bring on depression, despair, and defeat. That's why it is extremely important to *speak the Word of God*. Meditate on what is pure, lovely, and good; things that bring faith, hope and love. *"Our weapons are not carnal, but they are mighty in Christ to the pulling down of strongholds (2 Corinthians 10:4).*

What is a stronghold? A stronghold in your life will keep you bound, controlled, mastering your life for the purpose of bringing destruction. It could be fear, depression, addictions, phobias, etc. . . God gave us the weapons to destroy that first and foremost. God is our true Stronghold, lean on Him and He will deliver you. *"The Lord is my rock, my fortress, and deliverer; my God is my rock, in whom I take refuge, my shield and the horn of my salvation, my stronghold* (Psalm 18:2).

Weapon 7 - Pray In The Spirit: Lastly, pray in the Spirit on all occasions with all kinds of prayers and requests. If you remember, I shared my experience of receiving this gift. If you're not sure what I'm talking about, read *Acts*

2:1-4: "When the day of Pentecost had fully come, they were all with one accord in one place. And suddenly there came a sound from heaven, as of a rushing mighty wind, and it filled the whole house where they were sitting. Then it appeared to them divided tongues, as of fire, and one sat upon each of them. And they were all filled with the Holy Spirit and began to speak in other tongues, as the Spirit gave them utterance."

Trials have a way of making us feel like we may be at the end of our existence, as though our life may be over. Sometimes, you may even feel like there is no God or that He is cruel and mean. Don't believe the lie that either God doesn't care, He's punishing you or that He doesn't exist. He loves you with an everlasting love, Jehovah-Shammah, Jehovah is there. He is with you; He will never leave you, or forsake you. He is there.

My prayer for you is that you may gain strength through the Lord Jesus Christ so that you may be able to stand the test and gain the victory. Amen!

Question: Are you putting your armor on for the day of battle?

Thoughts to ponder on: Shine your light and don't be afraid to speak the Word.

Things to do: Study the armor of God

CHAPTER 12

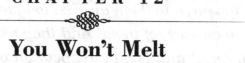

You Won't Melt

During this time of seeking God for our next move, our pastor's wife, Diane, read an article on a Chinese herbalist who specialized with hepatitis C. Don't forget, all conventional treatment failed, The Chinese doctor explained that because the liver was not exactly in the state of cirrhosis, the disease could possibly be reversed, that we wouldn't see results for about two to three months and that it would take time to lower the viral load. The doctor also explained that the herbs he would use works as a protector of the liver and has been known to lower your ALT levels. It also helps to block the production of free radicals called lipid. One ingredient that was in the medication while seeing the Chinese herbalist was Reishi mushrooms which have also been proven to help normalize liver enzymes and to help protect the liver. They may even help to restore a damaged liver. When seen by a Chinese herbalist you will use some of these herbs along with others that will be mixed in combination for your optimal health. Please be under supervised care when taking them.

He also explained we could lower the viral load and then maintain it from there. He also assured us we would never be able to get rid of the disease. Anytime someone spoke death over our lives, even if it was under our breath, we rebuked those words in Jesus' Name. At this time, we were seeing both conventional and Chinese herbalist. We went to the city every few weeks to be monitored by the medical doctor. He would take Joe's blood pressure, talk to us, and then send us home. There was nothing else that could be done.

Every time I left his office, I had a knot in my stomach and would have to encourage myself again with the Word. We were desperate and there was nothing the conventional doctor could do for us. Even though he was this sick, the doctor would not put Joe on the list to receive a liver because you have to have a certain meld score to be placed on the list.

One day while feeling like all hope was gone, I came inside our home after being out for a while and there was a message on the phone from the medical doctor. He explained in a puzzled tone of voice that Joe's blood work looks wonderful. He explained that the enzyme level was normal and not only that, his viral load was undetectable. I could not believe what I heard, I screamed on the top of my lungs, Joe! Come here quick! He came as fast as he could and after speaking to the doctor we were rejoicing and praising God. When we spoke with the doctor, he had no explanation for what had happened, he and the Chinese herbalist both confirmed they had never come across a report like this in thirty-five years' worth of work. The doctor agreed that it was a miracle.

We were ecstatic, the joy of the Lord was truly upon us, I began to make phone calls to everyone telling them of the miracle that had just taken place. What a testimony for people to hear, it encouraged everyone of the miraculous power of God.

I told everyone about this miracle to give God all the glory. I told people whether they wanted to hear it or not. I told neighbors, friends, and even strangers. The miracle was truly a blessing to all who heard. Our life almost went back to normal until. . . Joe had another blood test. We continued to praise God for his healing but unfortunately, his blood work did not come out the same as it had the month before. His body responded to the medication by showing undetectable levels not total eradication. The disease was never totally gone!

Talk about an emotional roller coaster. I went from blessing the Lord to wanting to run and hide from Him. There were days when all I wanted to do was hide under my covers and never come out to face reality. I wanted to run away from it all. I began to have feelings of despair and defeat. Feeling like I wished I had never been married or even had my children. My feeling of not wanting to be married or having my children was because they were so young and I didn't want them to suffer any more agony and mental pain. I had no song in my heart, and I didn't want to pray, I just wanted to vanish from the world.

I began to think of the pain and agony Christ suffered when He went to the cross, the separation He felt from

His Father and the words He screamed out "Why have You forsaken Me?" became so real in my heart. By no means, am I comparing myself to the Lord, but those words had such a profound impact on me. I began to feel forsaken and forgotten. I felt like my relationship with the Lord was shattered and my trust was broken. I heard those blood curtailing words.

WHY HAVE YOU FORSAKEN ME!

At the same time, this was happening, my great aunt, who was like a grandmother to me passed away, my father, was in the hospital having quadruple bypass surgery, and we were also dealing with Joe's health. So when Joe was not healed I took this so bad, because I truly believed the miracle had occurred. We were telling everyone that the Lord had healed Joe through this treatment and when this wasn't reality it really put me in a state of overwhelming sadness and depression. I had no energy, or desire to do anything! I felt this way for a few weeks; we were all exhausted mentally, emotionally, physically and spiritually. Even though Joe was weak he always took good care of his family. He told us to pack our bags and we all went on a cruise for a few days which was greatly needed.

On the Cruise

As I sat on the deck of the ship, the Lord began to search my heart and to remind me of His Word. Thank God for the Holy Spirit, who began to draw me back to Himself. *"O Lord, you have searched me and know me. You know when I sit and when I rise. You receive my thoughts from afar. You discern my going out and my lying down; you are familiar with all my ways. Before a word is on my tongue you know it completely O Lord. You hem me in-behind and before, you have laid your hand upon me. Such knowledge is too wonderful for me, too lofty for me to attain. Where can I go from your Spirit? Where can I flee from your presence? If I go up to the heavens you are there if I make my bed in the dawn, if I settle on the far side of the sea even there your hand will guide me and your right hand will hold fast to me. If I say, "Surely the darkness will hide me and the light become night around me even the darkness will not be dark to you; the night will shine like the day for the darkness is as light to you" (Psalm 139:1-12).*

According to a book I read from the Chinese herbalist we were seeing, Healing Hepatitis C by Qingcai, Zhang, M.D. "Interferon attempts only to eliminate the hepatitis virus and does not address the complicated problems of liver disease caused by viral hepatitis like inflammation which causes cirrhosis. Interferon is an anti-agent, and eventually, the body will produce antibodies against it. With long term use, hepatitis C virus will undergo heightened mutation creating more forms of the virus that may become Interferon-resistant. Which means the medication will not work to rid the disease. The other medication is Ribavirin which was developed in the late 1980's and when used alone it produces poor results. Ribavirin is toxic and can damage the liver. When used in combination common side effects of these nucleoside analogs are liver damage, elevated liver enzymes levels, jaundice, and fat deposits."[3]

I would like you to understand that taking the medication of interferon did make the virus undetectable

[3] Zhang, Qingcai, *Healing Hepatitis C: With Modern Chinese Medicine.* (New Yoprk:Sino-Med Institutue), copyright 2000. p.96-97

but never totally eradicated the virus. Doctors' orders were to stop using the Interferon and Ribavirin due to debilitating side effects that could have killed him. This is why my husband had to have his blood levels checked almost daily. The whole thing doesn't make sense to me; this medicine causes liver damage and raises liver enzymes! (For some people this treatment works and is tolerated, for my husband it didn't). We believe one reason why it didn't work is because he was already in stage 3/4 and he was treated aggressively. We continued using the Chinese herbs which did help Joe for a while. We continued with the regimen for a few more months then stopped because the liver was already extremely damaged.

Months after we were home from the cruise, I was again feeling so desperate because Joe was still so sick. I have flashbacks of being tormented while in my kitchen cooking a meal for my family. The girls and Joe were all in bed sleeping and a negative destructive thought crossed my mind about me and my family. Immediately, I knew where that filthy demonic thought came from and took authority over the devil in the Mighty Name of Jesus. "You filthy demon, the father of lies, I rebuke you in the Name of Jesus and by the power of His Blood!" It makes me shutter just to repeat what happened, but I want to be straight forward because I know the devil torments people, especially in situations like this and I want to share how I gained the victory. There have been many news reports of individuals killing their family because they were in a state of depression and saw no way out!

In our weakest point, that's when the devil brings thoughts of destruction that you can overcome! You could be minding your own business, and all of a sudden a destructive thought crosses your mind. It's not a sin to think those thoughts, but immediately throw them out! Don't entertain them. God gave us the power to overcome.

Don't forget, the devil even tempted Jesus, the Bible states *"The devil took Him to the holy city and had him stand on the highest point of the temple. If you are the Son of God, he said, "Throw yourself down, for it is written,*

"He will command his angels concerning you, and they will lift you up in their hands so that you will not strike your foot against a stone." Jesus also answered him, *"It is written: Do not put the Lord your God to the test"* (Matthew 4:5). Jesus used the Word of God to fight the thoughts and the enemy. You can do the same! *"Be self-controlled and alert. Your enemy the devil prowls around like a roaring lion, looking for someone to devour. Resist him, standing firm in the faith (1 Peter 5:8, 9).* Remember, he's like a lion. He roars a lot but has no teeth unless you let him.

My thoughts and mind tried to overtake me during this time of battle, I felt as though my family had been placed in a deep dark pit of fear. The only way out of this darkness was to hold on to Jesus, the light. God only knew my heart's desire and it was always to give Him all the glory, so that at the end of my test I may be as refined gold, ready for Him to use me.

I've heard people tell me that, the Lord won't give us more than we can handle. In my own frailty and weakness, I questioned God, "Are You sure You know what You're doing?" "I thought I could trust You, but the heat is so hot in my life, I feel like I'm melting and that my skin will literally melt off my bones." Have you ever felt that way? I'm sure you have, we all have trials we're going through.

I always ask my husband, "What do people do who don't have the Lord when they are in crisis situations?" I cannot imagine what it would be like not to have Jesus the Author and Finisher of my faith. The very one who holds the keys to life and death. Trust me; I know all about drinking your sorrows away, or taking drugs to numb the pain, I worked with the homeless for many years. We have to face life's challenges because we live in a fallen world, things will happen, but allow God to be able to use you while you're going through them. Don't allow yourself to become bitter, allow yourself to become better through life's situations.

Lesson # 4 It Is Not The Situation That Will Destroy You: I remember being taught while going to Bible School, it's not the situation that is going to destroy you, it is how you handle it. Begin to look at the glass half full instead of half empty. Take those situations you are in and begin to allow them to challenge you. How are you going to act?

Are you going to allow these circumstances to build your character into a Godly character?

Or are they going to destroy you? Are you going to allow the Holy Spirit to work through you while you are in the fire? Be patient and learn to take this opportunity to build you instead of break you. Allow the Holy Spirit to fill you. I must warn you though; you will have to go through the breaking process before the Holy Spirit can build you, and change you into His image. We sing songs in church, "Spirit of the living God fall fresh on me, break me, mold me, fill me and use me." Make sure you sing those words with a pure heart and get ready to be broken; then to be changed so He can use you.

Recently, I opened my devotional and God spoke clearly once again. I would like to share it with you; perhaps God will speak to you also.

Devotional: *You Won't Melt: Scripture reading Psalm 119:25-40.*

"Yes, there are times when you feel as though your very soul is going to melt as you boil in the crucible of testings. You don't even have hope to survive, the terrible fiery ordeal through which you are passing. All hope is gone; all dreams lie shattered at your feet. You feel disillusioned, disappointed, disgusted, betrayed, and deceived. Things couldn't be worse.

But my child, the truth is that things could be worse. You could be all alone in your crucible. You could be without My presence, without My Word to strengthen

103

you, and you could be completely out of My will. The heaviness and sadness through which you are passing cannot be permanent. I brought you into the fires, and I will bring you out. There are no powers strong enough to force you to stay in the fires when I see the work of grace has been finished in your life. I am doing a good work in you my beloved child. I am not melting away anything that is of value in your life, I am only melting out false relationships, unreliable confidences, fake friendships, unequal partnerships, pride, vanity, and boastfulness. I am melting the flesh realm out of your life, for I would have you be pure in Spirit, that you might see God.

Only the pure in heart shall see God. As I melt away all impurities, the veil between us disappear and you can see me, even your God, walking with you in the fires like I did with My three Hebrew sons who dwelt in captivity. Fear not to turn to My Word, for My Word which you are hearing now, will strengthen you to submit to the fiery trials that will only melt away the dross and the chaff out of your life. Your soul will never melt away in the fires; it will only be purified and made more beautiful and full of glory."

I felt all those emotions, disillusioned, disappointed, betrayed, forgotten, etc. . . . How right that passage is that states, things could be worse. The Lord has given us the ability to walk through this trial with His sustaining grace, joy, and victory. Although sometimes there are tears, He truly upholds our arms and gives us the courage each and every day. Behold, He is doing a new thing. When you go through the breaking process of purification don't run away from it, and don't try to make things go by quickly because sometimes you have absolutely no control over the situation.

Be teachable and honest with yourself, the Lord and others in your support circle. I know the Lord wants to bring us into new places in Him. We don't want to stay the same, our goal is that we want to be more like Him; so that in the process many will be healed and that we can come out as refined gold; anointed of God and ready to be used of Him.

Question: Are you going to allow your situations to build you or break you?

Ponder: The heaviness and sadness through which you are passing cannot be permanent. The Lord brought you into the fires, and He will bring you out.

CHAPTER 13

❖

The Fire

Bible Application: My husband and I have been feeling like the three Hebrew boys, Shadrach, Meshach, and Abednego. They declared boldly to the King that *"they would not serve him and they did not have to defend themselves because their God would save them from the blazing fiery furnace"* (Daniel 3:16-30). Their faith was strong and commitment to God was unshakable! They told the King that "if their God didn't save them from the flames, they would still not bow down and serve their gods or worship the golden image." What happened? Did God prevent them from being thrown in the fire? No! They were thrown into the furnace and Nebuchadnezzar turned up the heat seven times hotter than usual. Do you notice something?

A. **God Did Not Deliver Them From The Fire:** even though they declared boldly to the King that He would.

B. **The Lord Was With Them *"In"* The Fire:** When the King looked, he saw four men in the fire walking around and unharmed. I can't imagine they were just walking around, they were probably dancing and singing praises to God. That was how I was feeling; I knew God was with us in the fire

C. The Lord Allows Us To Be Placed In The Fire: but He does promise that when you walk through the flames you will not be burned. He will be right there with you to see you through and bring you strength and victory.

"When you pass through the waters, I will be with you; and when you pass through the rivers they will not sweep over you. When you walk through the fire, you will not be burned; the flames will not set you ablaze. For I am the Lord God the Holy One of Israel, your savior" (Isaiah 43:2-3).

We all know the end of the story, the Lord was with those three Hebrew boys in the crucible, they were not harmed, and not one hair was cinched on their head when they walked out of the furnace. They made up their minds to serve the Lord whether He delivered them or not. When the King realized they lived through what seemed to be a death sentence, the King, and the whole region bowed down and worshiped the Lord. God used that desperate situation to bring many to salvation and to glorify Himself.

The Word tells us *"In this world we will have tribulations, but be of good cheer for I have overcome the world"* (John 16:33). Many people seem to know that part of the Scripture, but let's take a look at what the

Scripture says before. He tells us we will have tribulation and to be of cheer. Jesus quotes, *"I have told you these things, so that "in Me" you may have peace."* Do you see it? Only in Him can we have peace, and then we are able to be of good cheer because we rely on God, our Father.

The correct way to read the scripture is, *"I have told you these things so that in Me you may have peace. In this world,we will have tribulation, but be of cheer for I have overcome the world" (John 16:33).* Suffering and tribulation will come, we live in this world of great sorrows, However, the Lord, tells us, to be of cheer, He has overcome the world.

That can really be hard when everything is turned upside down and you feel like the world in front of you is collapsing. Even though my world and my husband's world seemed as though it were collapsing, our minds were made up that we would look to Him in times of suffering. *"As for me and my house, we will serve the Lord" (Joshua 24:15).*

He promises that in Him we will overcome. Make up your mind to choose the Lord. I have seen my husband face death and still trust the Lord. How did he trust the Lord with his life? He chose to do that. Remember, you can choose life or death, blessings or curses, the choice is yours. A quote I heard from a speaker in Bible school was...

"Faith That Is Tried By Fire Is A Faith That Will Stand No Matter What God Will Or Will Not Do."

My husband knows God's love for him; therefore, he knows there is hope for his future. God's love is unchanging, His love is eternal, and His love will take away all our fear. "Perfect love cast out fear" and God is perfect love. He knows his purpose for living here on earth and that is to give God all the glory for everything you do and say even while going through your trials. Then at the end of our life, He may say, "Well done my good and faithful child. Come unto My banqueting table and sup with Me forever."

Can you imagine? The Word "forever" is a long time. You may live a ripe old age of about 90-95. Even if you live a few years after that, life goes fast. It's like a vapor; you're here one minute and gone the next. Everything you think that has some value to you here on this earth will be left behind for someone else to enjoy. Only those things we do for eternity will last forever. Your real life is where you spend eternity, guaranteed you will live forever, and where you spend it is totally up to you!

"For God so loved the world that he gave his one and only Son, that whoever believes in him shall not perish but have eternal life. For God did not send his Son into the world to condemn the world, but to save the world through him." (John 3:16,17).

Notice what you have to do? Believe on Him, and then you will not perish.

Question: Will you choose life today no matter what the situation you are going through?

_____

_____

_____

Ponder: If you are seeking peace, ask God to fill you with His eternal peace that the world cannot offer. You will be amazed that even though things may not change, your inner peace will strengthen you, so you can face anything with courage.

Peace I leave with you, not as the world gives...My peace is eternal

CHAPTER 14

Don't Be a Defeated Christian

Life Application: I can look back from the beginning of our journey, and say, "I have seen the **increase** of my maturity level, and that I have gained wisdom by going through the purification process." I know it's not finished and when this pruning season is over, rejoice because there will be another one. I can say there has been a tremendous **growth** in both myself and my husband in **faith, trust, and belief.** There is a sobering of life and clarity of what truly is important.

I like what King Solomon wrote in Ecclesiastes 2. All of it is meaningless! Don't get me wrong, I love having fun, I enjoy vacations and everything else life has to offer, I enjoy my home, family, and friends, and I love purchasing new things. However, I have experienced the frailty of life and that is, it rains on the righteous as well as the unrighteous. Just because you serve the Lord and have everything to live for, it doesn't mean you won't go through sickness or anything else that might try to prevent you from living life to the fullest. What I do want to tell you is, prayer can change things and God does hear the prayers of the saints. **He can add years to your**

life just because you prayed and this is what we believed for my husband. A total healing, that God would add many years to his life.

Bible Application: *"In those days, Hezekiah became ill and was at the point of death. The prophet Isaiah son of Amoz went to him and said, "This is what the Lord says, put your house in order because you are going to die, you will not recover." Hezekiah turned his face to the wall and prayed to the Lord. Remember oh Lord, how I have walked before you faithfully and with wholehearted devotion and have done what is good in your eyes. And Hezekiah wept bitterly." Before Isaiah had left the middle court, the word of the Lord came to him; Go back and tell Hezekiah, the leader of my people, This is what the Lord, the God of your father David says; I have heard your prayers and seen your tears, I will heal you. On the third day from now, you will go up to the temple of the Lord. I will add fifteen years to your life, and I will deliver you and this city from the hand of the king of Assyria. I will defend this city for my sake and for the sake of my servant David"* (2 Kings 20:1-6).

I love Hezekiah's reaction when Isaiah told him he had gotten a word from the Lord that he was going to die. It sounded pretty definite; after all, Isaiah was a prophet of the Lord. This just goes to show you God does hear your prayers, he didn't listen to his word, he went to God himself and the Lord heard Hezekiah's prayer. Go directly to God yourself and He will deliver you.

A. Stand In Faith: Stand in faith believing that He hears you and can turn things around. Always keep your heart toward God. King Solomon says it all, *"Fear God and keep His commandments, for this is man's all. For He will bring every work into judgment, including every secret thing, whether good or evil"* (Ecclesiastes 12:13).

In other words, what you do for eternity will last forever. What you do spiritually and for the Kingdom of God is where it counts. Don't be caught when God calls you home saying, Lord! Not yet, what have I done for You?

B. Take Every Opportunity: Take every opportunity now and complete what you know to do. The Bible says, "The days are evil but the harvest is ripe." Go into the harvest and reap those rewards. "The one who wins souls is wise." All you can take with you when this life is over are people. Don't allow yourself to be caught up in yourself while going through hard times. Reach out to those around you with an encouraging word or a helping hand. There are always people around you who are going through greater difficulties than yourself. Do what the scripture says, *"Comfort those around you with the same comfort that has been given you by the Holy Spirit"* (Corinthians 12:4).

C. Rise Above Those Emotions: Don't allow yourself to have a pity party, rise above those emotions and be a blessing to someone in need. I've seen Joe do that during his most trying times. Yes, there are times of feeling sad and feeling like what's the use of living, however, don't stay there. It's okay to go through those feelings, after all, we are human, but the key is not to stay there. I've seen Joe rise above those emotions and bless individuals with Godly wisdom.

"Store up for yourselves treasure in heaven where moth and dust do not destroy and where thieves do not break in and steal. For where your treasure is, there will your heart will be also" (Matthew 6:20, 21). Remember to "guard your heart for that is the wellspring of life."

What I mean by this is that when you're filled with Jesus and abiding in His will for your life, your heart will be filled with Him and there will be no room to hear the negative from those around you.

D. Don't Be A Defeated Christian: Be a Christian who is Christ-like and what did He do? He blessed those around Him, even His enemies. Be a blessing you can, even while you're going through the greatest pain in your life.

I can see the transformation that is beginning to happen in our life. There is still urgency in our spirits for my husband's total healing, but to go beyond that, there is urgency in our spirits to complete the call of God on our lives. There is an urgency to get the Gospel out and to tell the world time is short. There is life after death, and not only that, there is life and life more abundantly offered here, in this life, even while you're going through the most difficult time in your life.

Life Application: Jesus did promise, He would *"Never leave you or forsake you" (Hebrew 13:5).* I not only feel His hand extended but I can feel the grace to walk through this huge storm with victory.

There Is Victory For Us Even When We Face Life's Uncertainties and Challenges.

The grace that He bestows on us is His power to walk with joy and filled with peace knowing He will meet our daily need. Jesus said, *"My grace is sufficient for you" (2 Corinthians 12:9).*

I have come to the realization over and over again that I am nothing, I have nothing, and I can do nothing except through the grace and power of God that He bestows on me. His grace is made perfect in my weakness, and because of Him, I am more than an overcomer.

"Bestow on those around you the crown of beauty instead of ashes, the oil of gladness instead of mourning, and a garment of praise instead of a spirit of despair. Then you will be called oaks of righteousness, a planting of the Lord for the display of His splendor." (Isaiah 61:3).

Question: Are you abiding in Christ to the fullest? That's where faith comes in stronger!

_____

_____

_____

Ponder: Don't allow yourself to become bitter, become better through life's situations

CHAPTER 15

Keep Standing

Right now, there are no answers, both, conventional treatment and Chinese herbs failed; both treatments try to buy time for patients until another anti-viral treatment is available and unfortunately there is nothing!

However, Christ has kept us focused on Him. I'm going to take a few more minutes and share some of the continued truth that was and is our stability in which we stood and in which we were grounded.

Lesson #5 Speak The Word: I will continue to speak the Word over my husband. Why? **Jesus IS the Word.** *"In the beginning was the Word, and the Word was with God, and the Word was God. He was with God in the beginning. Through Him all things were made; without Him, nothing was made that has been made. In Him was the life and that life was the light of men. The light shines in the darkness, but the darkness has not understood it"* *(John 1:3).*

I will continue to speak the Word, which is, certain scriptures over my husband and I will not give up! I will take this opportunity and say, "Ok Lord, show Yourself to me and to my family."

A. **Don't Give Up!** If you want something bad enough you won't give up, you will continue to ask. Have you ever been around a child, when they want something they ask and ask and ask until finally you give them what they want? Jesus tells us, "Come as little children," simple faith. Seeking is something we need to do. Earnest petition along with obedience to God's will.

B. **Knock Continually:** When a child wants a door to open they will knock on the door continuously until finally that door is opened and they can walk in. In other words, persevere in prayer. If you notice, all of the things we are taught to do are continued action. Knocking implies perseverance to God even when He does not respond quickly.

Bible Application: Let's take a look at the woman with the issue of blood. She spent all she had on doctors and still nothing helped. One day she heard about Jesus coming to town. I can picture her intense desire to see the Lord. She ran down the road and saw the large crowd gathering around him. She wasn't moved by the large crowd that could have crushed her; she didn't give up and go home. She persevered through the crowd, pushed people out of the way until she was able to reach through the crowd. To reach through the crowd implies, she reached her hand around people enough to touch the hem of His garment. I picture this woman falling to the ground to touch the hem of Christ's garment.

The desperation this woman had was intense, it was her only hope of healing and health because nothing had worked and she was out of money. All of a sudden, it happened! She came up behind Him and touched the edge of His cloak. Immediately her bleeding stopped. Jesus stopped walking, turned around and asked, "Who touched me" (Luke 8:43-48). She was healed! The Bible states, "She was bleeding for twelve years and no one could help her, she spent all she had and nothing could be done."

When Jesus saw that power had gone from Him and realized it was this woman in desperation who touched Him, He told her "Daughter, your faith has healed you, Go in peace." He called her daughter, symbolizing God's heart for humanity. This woman finished her life strong, healed and full of God's loving kindness. She is a great example of faith, perseverance and longsuffering.

When life brings you challenges, stand your
ground for what you believe, don't be moved
by circumstances or by what people say.
Stand your ground and stand strong.

Finish Strong and Remember You Win
With The Lord No Matter What.
You Win!
Let Your Faith Be Your Motivator.

Question: What is your cross?

_____

Question: Are you willing to pick up your cross and walk in joy?

_____

Question: Will you listen to the voices of doubt and unbelief or faith and trust?

_____

Question: Will you continue to believe by faith when all your physical assets are gone

Or will you keep the faith knowing He is your answer?

_____

Ponder: The Lord is your strength, He will see you through.

CHAPTER 16

Praise Him Anyhow!

As I'm reminiscing about my own testimonies and writing about the lessons I have learned, I'm getting excited because I've seen His faithfulness. Do you notice something? I've been able to see His faithfulness only while going through these trials.

It's amazing that it's your trials and testing's that will give you a testimony. We love to hear the miraculous because it lifts our faith and encourages us to hold on and continue to believe. The only time we can receive a miracle is when we need one. It's hard to go through the fire and trials, but if we can only look with His eyes spiritually you will make it and become more than a conqueror.

Just last week while feeling sorry for myself, I asked the Lord "Why does my family always have to be picked on?" Sounds childish I know, but that's how I felt at that moment. I quickly changed my attitude and began to thank the Lord for what He will do. I began to give the Lord thanks for allowing us to go through this great trial. Believe me, it was only through the grace of God I was able to do that.

During this most difficult time in my life in 2003, my husband was unable to work for that year; at times, I felt like we were going to lose our home. God was faithful! He moved upon individuals hearts to bless us with monetary gifts; it takes several months to receive benefits from Social Security, we were praying we didn't have to move. We were willing to say good-bye to family and friends, we did not know the future and if we were going to be able to afford to live here on Long Island. However, God provided supernaturally to meet all of our needs.

One day, I said to my husband, "I have to go and get a job." I left and about half hour later I came back and told him I got a job at Tutor Time which is a center that cares for children ages birth-5. It was not the best paying job, but it was more than I had before and I was able to bring my children with me if I had to because they were also very young at that time. God also knew it was laying a foundation for a future promotion for my next place of employment.

During this time, we had to trust Him for everything. There were even days when I was the recipient of receiving food for my family from Hope For The Future. It was very humbling to be on the other side, but also, a tremendous blessing. Every day, God kept impressing the word *"trust"* in my heart.

Lesson #6 Trust: Trust is something we all long for, we want to be able to trust and we want people to be able to trust us. If you break trust you lose respect for each other and the relationship is broken. Relationships are built on trust, believing that there will be honesty, integrity, and loyalty to each other. Putting your faith in another person, and having confidence they will never let you down or fail you.

I'm not only discussing relationships with each other, I'm also referring to a relationship with the Lord Jesus. He is a personal God and wants that communion with you on a daily basis, which is called relationship. He wants you to be able to trust Him with your life. The scripture that comes to my mind is, *" For I know the plans I have for you, declares the Lord, plans to prosper you and not to harm you, plans to give you hope and a future"(Jeremiah 29:11).*

I will continue to trust God and praise His Holy Name because He loves me, and we have a relationship. I will not walk in fear; I will turn to my Rock who will supply my every need.

Bible Lesson: *"It happened after this that the people of Moab with the people of Ammon, and others with them besides the Ammonites, came to battle against Jehoshaphat. When Jehoshaphat heard this he feared, he did not allow the fear to control and overtake him instead he proclaimed a fast and set himself to seek the Lord.*

All Judah gathered together (the army of the Lord) to ask help from the God. Then God spoke and said, "Do not be afraid nor dismayed because of this great multitude (great trial) for the battle is not yours but God's. Position yourself and stand still and see the salvation of the Lord who is with you. Jehoshaphat stood and proclaimed what the Lord had told him. Believe in the Lord your God, and you shall be established; believe in His Prophets, and you shall prosper. When he consulted with the people, he appointed those who should sing to the Lord, and who should praise the beauty of holiness. As they went out to face the army, he placed the singers on the front line and as they sang, " Praise the Lord, For his mercy endures forever and began to sing and praise the Lord all the other armies began to fight against each other and the battle was won by Jehoshaphat and the Lords army" (II Chronicles 20:1,17,21,22).

A. **We Are The Lords Army:** We are the Lords army no matter what we are going through; praise the name of the Most High, He will deliver you. Sing and shout unto the Lord. Notice how Jehoshaphat did not allow his fear to control and overtake him? Instead, he called a. . .

B. **Fast To Seek The Lord:** Then the Lord spoke and told him not to be afraid, to stand still and to watch the salvation of the Lord. Remember the word "salvation" is to protect, deliver and to heal. Amen! They sang praises to God through their battle.

C. **Anchor Your Thoughts:** To prevent us from swaying emotionally we continued to hold onto scripture, and listen to Gospel music which anchored our thoughts around the Rock; which is Christ. Although our pain was emotionally too great!

We knew we had to sing and honor God.

Joe and I are committed to Him and we continued to praise the Lord even though it was very hard to see His plan for our lives. We knew God's grace was going to carry us; we relied on Him for everything and continued to trust Him.

It seemed as though there was nowhere to turn, except to God. Our pain was too much to bear. Even though we were hurting deeply, we continued to put on Godly music. We played music throughout our home and before we knew it, we were raising our hands to Jesus in a sign of surrendering to Him and His perfect will. Despite the outcome, but still trusting Jesus He was going to heal our home. *"The Spirit of praise does lift the spirit of heaviness" (Psalm 60).*

Something to do:

Put On Godly Music, Sing Your Heart Out and Get Ready To Defeat The Enemy!

One day while taking a shower the Lord impressed on my heart how many songs have been birthed through many trials and hardships. If you heard the testimony of many gospel songs they were written when facing huge trials. "It is well with my soul."

Is a perfect example, of a beautiful hymn that was written through a tragedy.

Notice how these great men of God sang through their great trials of life? You may not be able to sing right now, perhaps you are reading this book because you need comfort, strength, and direction for your life.

My Prayer For You: is that the Lord will give you the strength to put on Godly music that will uplift your spirit and cause you to sing even in the most difficult times. It won't change your circumstance, but it will change your emotions which give you the ability to think clearly and then it will change your circumstance as it did for Jehoshaphat.

Remember, give the enemy no room, no foothold. Your mind is the strongest battlefield. The devil loves to torment and bring thoughts of fear and death. "Satan has come to kill, steal, and destroy; but God has come to give life and life more abundantly."

Question: What are you dealing with today?

_____

_____

Question: What is the enemy using to destroy you?

_____

_____

Question: What do you need to be delivered from?

_____

_____

Lean On Him, The Strong Tower and
See Your Problems Change

"The name of the Lord is a strong tower; the righteous run into it and they are safe" (Proverbs 18:10). Blessed be the Name of the Lord,

CHAPTER 17

Believe For The Impossible

Nothing is impossible when you put your trust in God. Dare to believe the impossible. The impossible is, when man can't, God can! Believing for the impossible gives you an anchor to hold on to and wait with expectation. While I waited for my answer, my belief and faith gave me hope and a confidence for my future with my family.

For many years we trusted, held on to, and believed the Word of the Lord. A friend of mine, Evey, gave us a plaque for our home with the word "Believe" on it, every time I look at it, the plaque reminds me to believe and have hope. What a perfect gift! We believed for the impossible!

After Joe went through his treatment in 2003 and became deathly ill; seventeen months later he went back to work. Whenever someone asked me how Joe was feeling during that time, I always replied, he's doing well. He's working, looks good, has energy! Praise God he's doing well, I spoke by faith. We did everything we knew to do, so we rested in the Lord. What I mean by the word rest is that we trusted Him. We always had confidence the battle was the Lord's and not ours. During that time of resting in the Lord, we continued to walk by faith, not by sight. I heard a quote from Pastor Zarlengo who is the senior pastor of Smithtown Gospel Tabernacle, the church we attend

"Faith Compels You To Rest In The Midst Of Trials."

That is exactly what we did. It doesn't mean we stopped praying and pursuing our desire, it means that we gave up our expectations and time limit and totally surrendered to the Lord to be able to trust Him and believed that He would meet our every need. By this time, there were no treatments for Joe, and thank God, He gave us the ability to rest in Him.

Jesus wants all of us, not part of us. Those tests that you are going through are to see if you really mean what you say. I love you, Lord! Do you really? I trust you, Lord! Do you really? God tested Abraham and it was considered unto him as righteousness. Just think about it, his wife was barren for 90 years, they couldn't have any children, yet God promised him to be the father of many nations. He could have given up, but instead he believed, against all hope. He never gave up, he went off course a little bit, but God in His greatness and mercy brought him back and he was able to see the promise fulfilled.

We Believed Against All Hope That Our Promise Was Going To Be Fulfilled Too!

The Progression Begins

We continued to believe and stand in faith that God would miraculously heal Joe. Our fervent prayer and belief system held us together. Every time we heard a word about the Lord healing livers or hepatitis C, we claimed it for him. We continued to see the doctor but there was never anything they could do. There were no treatments for him and his blood work was always out of range, from 2003-2008 we focused on the Lord and His promises. *"I lift up my eyes to the hills-where does my help come from? My help comes from the Lord the maker of heaven and earth"* (Psalms 121:1).

Joe and I always tried to have fun with our daughters despite going through this trial. We took the girls and their friends to New York City for the weekend. We had a wonderful time and there were no complications until we sat on the train to go home. I looked at Joe's legs and noticed they were swollen, extremely swollen.

We were sitting diagonally from my girls, so I turned my face toward the window as tears ran down my cheeks. When we arrived home and their friends left, both Bethany, now 12, and Jessica, 9, cornered me and said, "Mommy, we saw you crying on the train. What is going on? I explained daddy's liver is beginning to fail in a greater way. I strongly believe we should be open and honest with our children; they are smarter than you think!

I also told them, we are continuing to believe God for healing which can happen in three ways. First, God can impart a new liver to daddy miraculously and he will be restored. Second, God can heal daddy by allowing him to have a liver transplant. This happens by getting a liver from a deceased person. Third, God can heal daddy by taking him home to Heaven where there will be no more pain, sorrow or sickness. We will bc united one day.

Jessica said, "Mommy I like it better the first way" and we hugged and cried together. Bethany lay quietly on her bed sobbing softly. I went over to her, stroked her hair and said, "Baby, tell mommy what is it that you're thinking, please talk to me." I waited a few minutes as she tried to talk in between her sobs and tears when she finally said, "How long does daddy have to live?" I kissed her and said, "I don't know, but I believe for a long time."

I left her room and found somewhere to cry myself. The Lord gave me His strength to tell the truth in love with firmness without having my feelings get in the way. That's again, the hardest thing I ever had to do, well, one of the hardest. If I allowed my feelings to take over I would have fallen apart and I refuse to do that!

When I think about how much our daughters have gone through it breaks my heart. I always continue to ask the Lord to keep them in His care and I know they will be strong women of God for everything they have had to endure. Thank You, Lord, for sustaining our girls with grace, Amen! *"The eyes of the Lord are on the righteous and His ears are attentive to their cry" (Psalm 34:15).*

In December 2007, while working, I received a phone call from my husband who told me he was gasping for air. He felt like he couldn't breathe. I rushed him to the hospital to make sure he wasn't having a heart attack. When the doctor took x-rays, they could see his lungs were filled with fluid and diagnosed him with walking pneumonia.

He had no fever, no cough; no symptoms at all just had difficulty breathing. The ER doctor told us to see a pulmonary specialist to have his lungs drained. I immediately called a specialist and the next day Joe had his lungs drained from all the fluid. The doctor explained the water was no longer in his lungs, it was now surrounding his lungs and he referred us to see our liver doctor.

That week we took the train to the hospital to see the liver specialist. When the doctor read the blood work, he handed a referral to us and said, "Now you can be placed on the list." We looked at each other in amazement and said to the doctor, "That's it? That's all you're going to do?" We were at a loss for words, Joe and I saw this doctor for five years thinking he was one of the best, going in and out of the city and nothing was ever done! He finally reached the number in order to even be considered to be placed on the list and as I learned while going through the process that doesn't mean much.

What it does mean, other organs are at a risk of failing. His number was 17, that means now you have to go through months of evaluations. If you don't pass these series of tests, you can be rejected to be placed on the waiting list to receive a liver. They will not consider you if you have cancer, smoke, drink, or any other major problems. This information I had to learn while going through the process, when my husband was in end-stage liver failure. No one explained the procedure to us, not even the doctor. I could go into some stories about having the wrong doctor but I won't, however, do more research and make sure you are seeing the correct one who truly can guide you to the end.

As we sat on the train on the way home after receiving the news of his meld score which was then five years since he was diagnosed, I felt so many emotions going through my head and heart. I have to admit, I was looking at every man that walked on the train and I felt jealous of their good health and strength. I couldn't understand how the Lord was allowing this to take place with a man who loved and honored Him and had everything to live for.

I could feel anxiety trying to attack me; at times, I felt light headed and even nauseous. It all felt like I was living through a dream, a bad dream. Joe and I just sat closely together as we tried to be a support to each other. I felt so helpless, but together we continued to rebuke every negative report.

Every day we continued to pray over him and believe for a miracle as we also encouraged each other emotionally. He was going through anxiety about dying and leaving his family. It was so hard because every day we were looking death square in the face. Yet we still had to function because we had two young daughters who needed us.

We know there is healing in the Lord's Supper; so once or twice a week we took communion together and thanked the Lord for His broken body and blood He shed for us. I also anointed him with oil often and prayed over him. We did everything we knew to do and continued to believe God.

By April 2008, Joe seemed to be losing his muscle mass, not realizing he was having what's called "muscle waste." It's when your body begins to eat itself from all the protein. To the best of my understanding of what the doctors were telling me, protein intake is extremely important for people with cirrhosis of the liver. Too much protein can increase ammonia levels in the blood, too little protein can slow the process of healing of the liver. Please be under a specialized care of a nutritionist who can give you the best diet possible.

During this time, it was the craziest thing, everything began to happen right before our eyes, yet we didn't really see it. I explain it like a baby. When my daughters were born they were so tiny, 5 pounds, little by little they began to grow right before our eyes, yet we didn't see it. In this case, it was reverse; he was wasting away, little by little, right before our eyes. Malnutrition is also common with the virus of hepatitis. When this was happening to Joe, we thought it was because he wasn't exercising and getting older. We also noticed his skin was beginning to take on a darker shade.

Beginning Signs Of Liver Failure

Even through this, we still declared, God is faithful in all His ways and will lead His children to the end! One day I was talking to a friend who I highly respect in the medical field, Pete, and he told me about a liver doctor who sounded great. I changed doctors and brought Joe to see this new doctor in May. His two sisters, younger brother Diego and parents went with us for support. The doctor examined Joe and agreed his legs (edema) and abdomen (ascites) were beginning to hold fluid. This condition is from increased pressure in the veins entering the liver which is called, portal hypertension. The doctor asked many questions, everything seemed to be fine. His ability to work was normal, so he told Joe to go home and walk. "Do as much walking as you can."

At this point, he also had two hernias and the doctors would not operate due to his failing liver. However, the hernia could strangle him and he could also die from that. Everything was going against us! The doctor scheduled Joe to begin the tests to be placed on the liver donor list.

Even though we were living through this illness and diagnoses we still trusted the Word of the Lord. Hearing the doctor, but knowing, God is our Great Physician.

Against All Hope, We Continued To Believe.

Even though we believed for health, and the supernatural, by June 2008 we noticed significant changes in Joe's appearance. As I explained before, he lost his muscle mass; his legs and stomach began to hold water to the point he looked like he was expecting. Expecting what? I don't know! His body temperature became severely cold. If you remember, I mentioned his body temperature was always hot, having cold hands and feet are the beginning signs of liver failure. He was losing so much weight he needed to wear suspenders to hold his pants from falling because he couldn't wear a belt due to the swollen abdomen.

I think about the days I ran downstairs to read a book about cirrhosis of the liver. He began getting all the symptoms. Dark circles under his eyes, cold feet, and hands, swollen abdomen etc. During this time, we had to go back and forth to the doctor and have several outpatient procedures done.

I still remember vividly one of our hospital visits. Joe and I were walking on the sidewalk to get to the hospital, he could barely walk. He was using a cane to help himself when he picked it up and began to smash the garbage can that was on the sidewalk. I knew he was going through such deep torment, frustration, and anger at his condition.

It scared me at first to see him in this state, but I gently took his hand and guided him to the doctor's office. God gave me the ability to love him stronger, and understand what he was feeling. The agony and pain mentally, physically and spiritually was overwhelming. That moment was a huge release for him and never reacted like that again.

It was now July, I and everyone was noticing he wasn't looking good at all. He went from looking bad to worse, what's amazing is my husband, he got up and went to work every day to support his family, feeling like and looking like death. Even his co-workers and boss were amazed at his commitment. We went to our church picnic on July 4 and it was extremely noticeable he was dying. By this time his stomach was extremely extended, his temple had indentations on both sides. Typical look for people with cirrhosis of the liver and he was weighing about 135 pounds, normal weight is 175.

My Journal: A few days ago, July 17, 2008, was Jessica's 10 birthday. We had a celebration at my brother and sister-in-law's house, although Joe was too sick and not able to attend.

My Journal: Today is July 23; he was not able to go to work today. When I told him I would see him after I returned from work, and he asked me to stay home with him, I knew he wasn't feeling well. He saw the doctor for a few more procedures the next two days. I packed his bags to stay overnight in the hospital, but the doctor sent him home.

I was shocked because he looked so bad, but the doctor felt he wasn't ready and wanted to make sure he didn't get a staph infection.

We took a limousine to the hospital because by then, he was too sick to take the train. On the way home driving through the expressway I noticed his skin color was looking kind of orange. It was getting dark out and the street lights were beginning to go on so I felt like my eyes were playing tricks on me. It was no trick, he was truly turning orange, a faint tint of it on his olive complexion.

Encephalopathy (confusion and memory difficulties) is a brain dysfunction which someone can go through at end stage liver failure. Taking lactulose is crucial to rid the body of toxins at this point, a medication our doctor never prescribed to us. Therefore, I will describe what happened when Joe did suffer from brain confusion (encephalopathy).

By Saturday the 26 he seemed to be doing okay, a little weak, but stable. His two sisters, Rosa, and Maria came over and we all went to a health food store to buy him certain foods to eat. While he was in the store, he had to run out and sit in the car; he was beginning to feel weaker.

Joe a Few Days before Liver Failure

Sunday morning July 27 I knew I had to get him to church for prayer. Arrangements were made a few days before for all the pastors to be available to pray over Joe. I dressed him and literally brought him to church, had him prayed over, then I brought him home to be placed back into bed. He was that sick.

When I brought him to the prayer room he was beginning to seem lethargic. No one explained to me what to expect when someone goes into complete liver failure. That afternoon, his youngest brother, Jimmy, and his wife came to visit Joe and me. One hour after they left I noticed Joe walking in the living room. At first, I didn't think anything was wrong because the doctor had told him to walk, but I noticed he was almost in a trance while walking. He was walking back and forth, quickly.

I asked him if he was okay, and he replied, "yup, yup, yup, I'm fine, I'm fine, I'm fine, I'm going to bed!" He left the room to lie down. I thought to myself "that's weird; he never spoke like that before." I immediately called the doctor. Unfortunately, our doctor that we had seen just two days before was out of town and I spoke to another doctor who did not know Joe's medical history.

He didn't seem to be alarmed, I told him he was resting and he had to go for an endoscopy in the morning. I asked if it would be okay for him to rest so he will be prepared for the morning since the hospital was so far away. The doctor said it was fine, but if anything happens to call him. I looked at Joe, he seemed to be sleeping,

It was 11:30 p.m. I was exhausted from the day. As I rested my head on the pillow, I heard that familiar, gentle, but strong voice of the Holy Spirit say, "Wake up and look at your husband." My mind was fighting; I just wanted to close my eyes and go to sleep, but again, that still quiet voice within my heart, got a little stronger than the first time and said, "Look at your husband." While forcing myself to turn around and open my eyes, all of a sudden he jumped out of bed and stood up! I jumped out of bed and ran to him; he didn't know where he was or what he was doing. I pushed him down on the bed, ran to the phone and called his brother, Carlos. Twenty minutes later Carlos came, we picked him up and put him in the car. I could not call an ambulance because they would have taken me to the nearest hospital; I knew I had to get to New York-Presbyterian.

Joe's eyes were rolling behind his head; he was going into a coma. I brought a wet cloth with me, as his brother drove the car to the hospital, I dabbed his face with the wet cloth to keep him awake. Every time I dabbed his eyes, he hit his face and said, "Stop it!" My parents came rushing over to care for our daughters. Thank God this happened at night, if it took place during the day it could have taken two hours or more to get to the hospital.

On July 27, at 1:30 a.m. we arrived at the emergency room. They immediately hooked him up to all kinds of machines; he was going into a coma from liver failure. His eyes and skin were bright orange. His body was being poisoned from all the toxins.

The doctors immediately injected him with lactulose. Remember, this helps the body to release the poisons, if I had this medicine to begin with at home, he would have never gone into complete liver failure from toxins and ammonia poisoning his brain. If you have cirrhosis of the liver or know someone who does, please make sure you inquire about this medication, it could prevent further complications.

After the doctors were finished with that procedure they immediately placed him on a respirator because he was having trouble breathing. It was about 1:45 a.m. when his other four brothers, two sisters, and parents came rushing to the hospital. Everything happened so fast, I remember all the doctors rushing and moving so quickly. They knew exactly what to do, after a little while I asked the doctor if he was going to be okay, their answer was "I don't know, I hope so, but he may not come out of this." There have been cases that people remain brain dead or die at this point.

Joe was in such a state of mind that he does not recall anything. Praise God for His power and leading of the Holy Spirit, I stood face to face with the spirit of death. I looked into those bright orange eyes and spoke the Word of God directly to the illness.

"You filthy Spirit of death, I rebuke you in the Name of Jesus. You will not die but live and proclaim what the Lord has done. Loose him in the Name of Jesus."

I also stood around the bed with his family and I asked them to hold hands and pray with me. I recall one sibling saying, "It's not working" and I said, "I know, but it will, I know it will." About one hour later, I found a poster with pictures of a nurse, an apple, a bathroom and so forth and showed it to Joe. Don't forget, he was on a respirator and couldn't do anything. As I named the pictures, I told him to point to the correct one. He struggled to lift his hand and could barely point with his finger; amazingly he did and was correct on all the

142

answers. I knew he wasn't going to be brain damaged. Praise the Lord!

After a while in the ER, we had to wait in the waiting room while the doctors completed some tests. All I could do while in the waiting room was to lie on the bench and cry. I sobbed by myself and then got up and went into the hall. I noticed a woman pacing the floor and said to her "you look like me, are you waiting for a family member?" She told me her husband was in the operating room having a liver transplant. I explained to the woman that my husband will need one and she talked to me for over two hours.

All of a sudden a door swung opened and the surgeon walked out and spoke to "Sue." I was shocked as I stood in the middle of the conversation between the surgeon and "Sue" they were talking with ease and assurance that everything went well, I was in amazement.

They had such a wonderful rapport with each other, it seemed as though they were reminiscing about a great event. I immediately introduced myself to the doctor when they were finished with their conversation. I explained my husband is in need of a liver transplant and I asked for his business card and he handed one to me and walked away. In that short time I knew I wanted that doctor to do the surgery, he seemed so confident. He also told me there are many wonderful doctors and you could not ask for a certain one. When I was able to see Joe again it was about 6:00 a.m. we stayed with him around the clock. Thanks to his family and my parents who cared for Bethany and Jessica, Joe was never left alone.

CHAPTER 18

❦

Stretching My Faith

My mother being the church deaconess called the prayer line and people began to pray and fast for Joe's recovery. Joe's brother Jim also contacted Pastor Cymbala from the Brooklyn Tabernacle and asked for his congregation to keep Joe in prayer. I also called my mother's sister Liz from Texas and asked her to pass the word to my family about Joe's condition. She gathered all the information and asked her friends and family to pray. There were many people around the country who prayed continually. Joe also remembers people coming to his bedside to pray for him that he didn't even know. They heard about him from a local church and went to lay hands on him for recovery. Thank the Lord!

My Journal: July 29 the respirator came off and he was placed on an oxygen mask. Today is day three in the hospital July 30. So much has happened, praise God! Joe is not brain dead; we have a lot of obstacles to overcome but I know we will by God's strength and power.

My Journal: August 2, he left ICU, the oxygen mask came off and he was placed on the sixth floor, he only had oxygen in his nose. Thank God for his family, they are a great support to us. One family member is staying with him so I'm able to go home.

When I went home, the first place I went was my church, Smithtown Gospel Tabernacle. There was a prayer meeting going on, they all welcomed me as we stood in faith and prayer for him. They handed me a prayer cloth that was bathed in prayer, this cloth was used as a point of contact for God's intervention. God was even stretching my faith by using the prayer cloth; I was willing to do anything. *"God did extraordinary miracles through Paul so that even handkerchiefs and aprons that had touched him were taken to the sick, and their illnesses were cured and the evil spirits left them"* *(Acts19:11).*

I could not wait to place the cloth on Joe and see the miracle. I went home from the prayer meeting, saw my girls, got a change of clothes, and the mail. To my surprise, in a large envelope was another prayer cloth from my mother's brother John and his prayer team from Texas. What a blessing, the Holy Spirit was confirming His power and ability to perform the same thing across the country.

I drove back to the hospital, and when I arrived, I showed Joe the two prayer cloths. We wrapped them around his arm after laying them across his chest thanking God for His miraculous power. "Lord, Thank

You for these cloths that are bathed in prayer, may all the faith be placed on my husband to bring him healing in Jesus' Name." Joe's hands and feet have been ice cold and they are warm, his eyes went from bright orange to pale yellow. "Praise You, Jesus, I glorify You Lord and by Your stripes, Joe is healed."

My Journal: Today is August 3, another emotional day. Bethany and Jessica came to the hospital for the first time today. Six days before Bethany's thirteenth birthday. They came with my parents and were brought by my friend, Debbie. When Bethany saw her father she sobbed so hard, my heart was broken and screaming again as I watched the look on my girl's faces. "Lord, this is not fair!", "My girls are going through too much!"

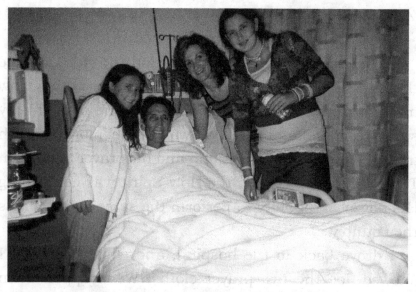

Hospital Visit by Daughters

We tried to make the best of the situation and sat Joe up in a chair and gave him a haircut. (I have a cosmetology license from High school.) The girls felt slightly better seeing him do that. God always gives me the courage and the strength to stand strong to be able to encourage our daughters so that they may learn to stand in faith for their father. Somehow, through it all, the Lord always put a smile on my face. Even in my deepest sorrow and pain.

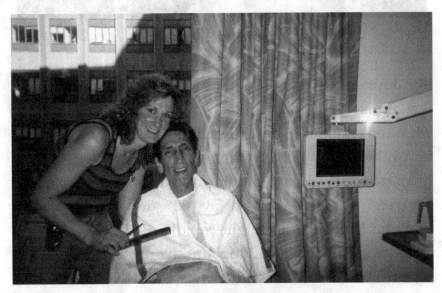

Giving Hair Cut

After the Hair Cut

My Journal: Today, August 4, he passed the swallow test, Praise God! Thank You Lord! He began to get hungry; who am I kidding, he was telling me he was starving and if he didn't get anything to eat he was leaving the hospital! He could not eat for three days which is bad for a person who is wasting away; he's down to about 118 pounds. He is losing weight rapidly. His lung collapsed today from the fluid buildup, and he needs to be tapped again. The fluid in his abdomen is about six liters. Every time they do this procedure we both cringe. They have to take a very long needle and place it in his back to drain the fluid. Last night his oxygen level dropped, the doctors don't like to tap him so much because an infection could set in. Every time they do that procedure he has to sign a release form.

Rosa, his sister, and I began to speak to the psychiatrist of the liver team while Joe was going through more tests.

She explained that we could possibly place him on an extended donor list; we both agreed that was a good idea. Anything to hurry the process; by now his meld score was about a twenty-one. Remember, his other organs are at risk. An extended list is not only from a deceased person but one who may have died from other complications like cancer. The psychiatrist also wanted us to attend meetings to learn about liver transplants.

One day, while I was trying to find the meeting I was to attend, I opened the door of a conference room and several men were sitting around a table. We introduced ourselves, and they told me they were a team of men who visited the patients to encourage them. I gave them Joe's information and they began to visit him. They themselves were recipients of a liver transplant. I thanked them and left the room so that I could find the class I was supposed to attend.

My Journal: Today is August 5, Joe has to have a biopsy for ulcers they discovered when he had the endoscopy. I pray they are not cancer; if they are, the doctors will not give him a transplant. Praise the Lord, the doctor said the ulcers are smaller than they thought, they do not look like cancer, but we have to wait for the report. They also found he has a small hole in his heart and are hesitant about operating.

My Journal: August 6 was Joe's first day out of bed. He's beginning to use the toilet, things you take for granted. The drain was removed out of his stomach,

My Journal: August 7, Praise the Lord, there is no cancer! Thank You Jesus! A doctor came to ask questions regarding the hole in his heart. We didn't even know he had a hole in his heart this was astonishing news to us. The doctor asked him if he ever played baseball and he has, so he didn't seem concerned that the hole would complicate the surgery. Every day there is a new miracle. I remember Pastor Zarlengo praying, Lord, Thank You for healing Joe even if it's step by step. That seems to be what's happening, Thank You Lord I will praise You, You're praise will continually be in my mouth. I will Bless You at all times, Your praise will continually be in my mouth. I Love You, Lord.

My Journal: Today August 9, I left the hospital to go home and celebrate Bethany's 13 birthday. It was a beautiful day, and I was trying to have fun, although there was a pain so deep within my soul because miles away lay my husband in a hospital bed waiting to either die or receive a liver transplant.

The Miracles Of Gods Provision During Many Years Of Constant Suffering Was Miraculous.

The Lord has blessed our coming and going. Before we knew how sick Joe was we began to refinish our kitchen, driveway, and landscaping. I told you, we always tried to live life to the fullest. No sickness or disease is going to run our home. Before I had to rush Joe to the hospital we were in the process of tearing down our cabinets, and then it all began. When I came home in between hospital stays there were workers at our home painting and completing the kitchen and driveway.

At night, I went outside and look up towards the Heavens and cried out to the Lord, "I don't understand! We have wanted to finish our kitchen for years and now that we're able to do this, my husband is dying? I don't understand!" After my natural self-spoke, my spirit man would take over and say, "Thank You, Lord, for Your provision in all things, I love You." The Lord spoke to my heart and said, "Wait and see, I'm doing this for a reason, your husband will come home." A peace would come over me and I would kiss my daughters and go to bed. The Lord gave me supernatural strength and comfort to run the house on my own. I thought about all the single moms in the world, my heart goes out to all of you. You are tough women and overcomers with the help of our Lord.

Joe spent three weeks in the hospital and completed all his testing's to able to be placed on the transplant list. Now it's just waiting time, waiting for a liver to become available. The thought of someone dying so my husband can live and receive a liver is mind boggling. Someone's pain would be my joy. Then again, there are millions of people who die daily, and their families are courageous and loving to donate their loved one's organs to save lives. Thank-you, from the bottom of my heart.

Joe's parents visited him every day and his father would sit at his bedside and say, "I'm here to comfort you, instead you are comforting me." His father would always say, "No son of mine is going before me." "Stay strong son, stay strong, God is not finished with you yet, in no time at all, this will be a memory for you to use to help others. The Lord loves you so much and He's not going to let you go, He is not finished with you yet."

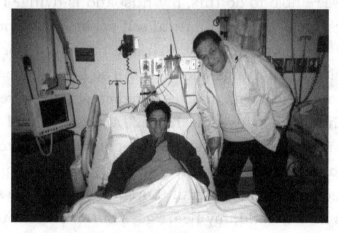

Joe and His Father

Joe held on to the Word of the Lord and really prepared for anything. At this time, he didn't know if the Lord was calling him home. He always made sure his heart was in right standing before the Lord. He told all the nurses and those who cared for him about Jesus, the Messiah.

Rosa and I discussed the possibility of her taking Joe home when he would be released from the hospital. She wanted to care for her brother while he waited for the phone call to receive a liver. She lived closer to the hospital in case of an emergency and was able to care for him in a greater way than I ever could. September is coming soon and the girls have to begin school in a few weeks; school?

I can't imagine sending my girls to school! Lord help like I don't have enough on my plate. Bethany is now entering the eighth grade and Jessica is in her last year of elementary, fifth grade.

CHAPTER 19

Keep Your Eyes Fixed

The day we all waited for finally arrived, August 17; Joe left the hospital, what a day of rejoicing for all of us. He left with an oxygen tank to help him breathe and weighing about 119 pounds. He had to learn to walk before he left the hospital. With determination and a good coach, he did it! At one point when he was walking in the halls, he was so skinny his sweat pants dropped to the floor, embarrassing! He told the three nurses, "Turn your head, I'm a married man." We had to laugh about everything. Don't forget, laughter is like medicine to the soul.

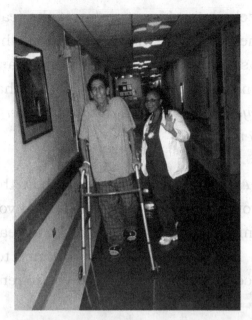

Learning to Walk

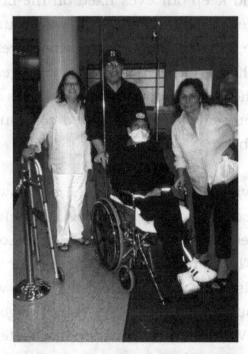

Leaving the Hospital With Siblings

A few weeks later, I went to "meet the teacher" night and explained what was happening in our home. Every year Joe was always with me, this year I was alone. The Lord kept impressing on me the scripture that says *"Let us fix our eyes on Jesus, the author and perfecter of our faith" (Hebrew 12:2a).*

Lesson #7 Are You "Fixed?" Notice how the scripture says keep your eyes fixed on Jesus. When you are fixed you are firmly rooted and attached; not easily moved or shaken. Being fixed causes you not to give into circumstances around you; it helps you to remain steady and stable.

We should keep our eyes fixed on the Lord because your eyes see many things that can sway your faith. Your eyes are the window to your soul which eventually will affect your heart, either positive or negative. "It doesn't look good, there is no hope." When your eyes are fixed on the Lord, you see with His eyes and continue to believe the impossible.

When I visit my husband and I see how weak and sickly he looks, I am able to look beyond that and keep my eyes and thoughts fixed on the Lord and His promises. "Thank You Lord that you care for us and Your love abounds." At one time I told the Lord, with all due respect, "You want me to trust You? I'm going to hold You to Your Word because Your promise states, *"So is My word that goes out from my mouth it will not return to Me empty, but will accomplish what I desire and achieve the purpose for which I sent it" (Isaiah 55:11).*

If your heart is not fixed you will soon give up and walk in defeat. Make up your mind to be fixed in your heart.

Devotional: "So today, as you set your heart to be fixed to do My will in a difficult task, know that the miracle of tomorrow will take place because of your strong attitude of determination in your heart today."

My Journal: God is so good, He encouraged me today by giving me this promise, and I never saw it before. *"Blessed is he who has "regard" for the weak; the Lord delivers him in times of trouble. The Lord will protect him and preserve his life; he will bless him in the land and not surrender him to the desires of his foes. The Lord will sustain him on his sickbed and restore him from his bed of illness" (Psalm 41:1-3).*

This verse was so encouraging to me. Joe and I both had regard for the weak when we worked with the poor. We helped them for many years; showing respect and dignity. I believe God will impart His life to him and restore Joe from his bed of illness. I will hold on to this promise and wait to see him well again. I believe His Word!

Every Friday, the girls and I packed the van and drove to New Jersey to visit daddy. The girls loved to go to see their father and visit with family.

Visiting Daddy

His two sisters and their families live in New Jersey. Rosa rented a hospital bed to help him feel comfortable. When we arrived he would be lying in bed resting or in pain with his legs. We spent hours rubbing his legs from cramps and chronic pain. Even though he felt like this, he always made an effort to get up and take us out. We would go to the stores, or out to eat, as long as he had all his medications, his cane to walk, the oxygen tank and one other paraphernalia, his pillow. He was skin and bones! His body looked like someone you would see in a concentration camp; an extended abdomen and skinny legs and arms. His thigh was the size of my arm! Despite any obstacles, we always made the best of any given situation. After the weekend, we would pack our bags and head home for another school and work week.

Before I continue with my story, I want to give you an explanation as to what will occur in my next few pages. Because Joe had severe cirrhosis, end-stage liver failure, his liver was becoming hard like a rock and blood flow was not able to filter properly, so high ammonia levels and toxins were poisoning his brain. When these compounds reach the brain, they cause a condition called hepatic encephalopathy. This is what took place the first time when he was going into a coma and again a few weeks later.

One night when I was home I received a phone call from Rosa. She and Maria were in the car on the way back to New York-Presbyterian Hospital because Joe was not talking right. By now he was taking lactulose, but his body was still being poisoned from the toxins. I called my parents which were about 2 a.m.; both my parents came rushing over. My mother stayed with the girls and my father drove with me to the hospital.

When we reached the hospital and went into the ER, Joe was lying on the bed unresponsive. He lay on the bed for about one hour like he was sleeping. I've heard stories of people being able to hear when they were spoken to, so I spoke softly into his ears. "Hi, sweetheart, I love you." I prayed over him and left the room to visit with my dad. Not everyone was able to be in the ER.

A little while later when I went back in to see him, he was up but speaking extremely erratic. He didn't make sense at all; he was calling everyone "Digo."

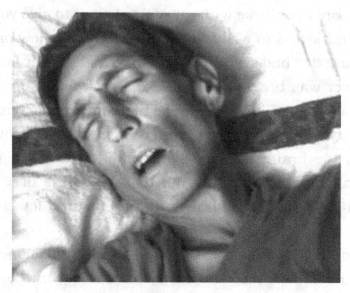

Joe Unresponsive

His younger brother's name is Diego. He looked at his sisters with a blank stare and called them Digo. When I walked in the room he blew me kisses almost like he knew who I was. In fact, I know he knew me because I was the only one he did that too. He turned and looked around so quickly and repeated himself every half of second. "Where am I?" I told him, "you're in the hospital." He would say, "Oh, why? What happened?" I would tell him, "We had to bring you back" and he would say, "Oh shoot, shoot, and ask why? Where am I?" He repeated himself like that for four hours. After staying with him for that time, I left the room to see my dad for a while and when I returned, Joe was sitting up in bed and looked at me and said, "Hi Babe" soft and sweetly like he always did. I screamed, "You're back! Praise the Lord, you're back! Thank You Jesus."

The next day around 10:00 a.m. he was returned to the 6 floor for some more evaluations. When they took his meld score again, they noticed instead of it going up which would be death, or close to it; and then they would be able to give him a liver (possibly), the level was lower. He was a sixteen, even lower from the time he arrived. Rosa took such good care of him; and of course the prayers, his score was going down. This is good in one respect but bad in another. You see, to receive a liver from the list you have to be at least a thirty-five which means at that point you may need a kidney transplant as well as a liver.

According to United Network for Organ Sharing, (UNOS), meld is a numerical scale, ranging from 6 (less illness) to 40 (gravely ill) that is used to allocate deceased donors. It gives each individual a scale based on how urgently he or she needs a liver transplant within the next three months. A patient's score may go up and down over time depending on the status of his or her liver disease. The problem is if the score is too high then the patient is critically ill and is in need of a whole organ instead of part. This is why the deceased liver is great because the patient can either receive the whole liver if needed or it can be split in half or thirds for other recipients.

If the recipient's number is really high then the person is put on status 1 for the urgency. A huge problem is, there are not enough livers to go around this is why many people die while waiting. In New York City alone in 2008, there were 19 people a day dying while waiting for a liver transplant.

Meld Score

According to a pamphlet I read at the hospital, from UNOS, the meld score is based on three areas

* Bilirubin: measures how effectively the liver excretes bile.
*INR (prothrombin time) measures the livers ability to make blood clotting factors
* Creatinine: measures kidney function. (Impaired kidney function is often associated with severe liver disease) This system was developed to determine who would die sooner while waiting for a liver. MELD means Model for End-Stage Liver Disease. [4]

After another two week stay, he was released and went back to live with his sister and brother-in-law in New Jersey. At this point, it was very critical to watch Joe and continue to keep him healthy enough for transplant when we received the phone call.

The whole process has to be accomplished in a timely manner, which is most critical. Even going through this, you have to use wisdom. My husband was on liquid restriction because then he had to be tapped (drained from fluid) and that procedure was also dangerous. One day during his hospital stay, someone told him "Don't worry about being tapped even though it's a risk, take

[4] Pamphlet: <u>Questions and Answers for patients and families about MELD and PELD UNOS Donate Life,</u> Richmond, VA:

care of your kidneys and drink water as needed." He did drink liquids, not as much as usual but more than he should have and I know this saved his kidneys.

While at Rosa's house, she was feeding him nutritious meals trying to keep him healthy to receive a transplant. However, Joe was extremely exhausted, physically, spiritually and emotionally. His mind was being tormented with thoughts of suicide. He thought about going to the store nearby to purchase a gun. Then, when no one was home or with him, he would walk in the woods and blow his brains out. It gives me the chills even writing about it. But this is reality!

Sometimes his thinking became foggy because of the pain he was in, and then eventually He would come out of this thought and ask God for forgiveness and strength to overcome. He fought those thoughts by holding onto the Word of God and the hope of getting a new liver.

He also reminded himself that if he did this, Heaven would not be his home and that he would miss entering the Kingdom of God. Remember, Satan is crafty and wants to kill and destroy! *"Don't you know that you yourselves are God's temple and that God's spirit lives in you? If anyone destroys God's temple, God will destroy him; for God's temple is sacred, and you are that temple"* *(1 Corinthians 3:16).*

He told himself this is not an option and God gave him the grace and endurance to be patient. You can truly see how the enemy was working overtime to discourage us and bring destruction. Please note, that if someone you know committed suicide, God knew their heart and

He has the final say to their life. He is a compassionate Father and has mercy on His children.

Things to do: If you ever have thoughts of suicide, immediately expose them by calling on the blood of Jesus and telling the closest person to you.

CHAPTER 20

❖

I Am Not An Option!

Sometime in September, Joe had to return to the hospital because he couldn't breathe again. His lungs were filling with fluid and needed to be drained. He was there for another week. I didn't stay every day because our children were in school and I had to work. I have to take a minute and let you know what a blessing my job is. Now I know why the doors opened for me to work at SCS, everyone has been such a support for me through this stressful time in my life. I work for Smithtown Christian School which is located in my home church Smithtown Gospel Tabernacle, so it is perfect! Thank you for your prayers, love and concern.

When I went to visit Joe, I walked into the hospital room and heard people discussing being a live liver donor. It was my first time ever hearing of such a procedure, none of the doctors we had seen previously had told us about living donation. When I walked in the room and heard about this procedure fear gripped me and I said, as everyone was looking at me. "I'm not to be considered, I have two children to raise, I am NOT an option!"

I walked out of the room, and down the hall as his sibling followed me and said, "What are you going to do? Let him die?" I said, "That's not up to me!" I stayed around for a while and spoke to the doctors. They told me not to worry because they like to check family members first. I thought "okay, Thank-God, he has seven siblings." I left the hospital after a while and went home to see my girls while Joe's family stayed with him.

As I was driving home and thinking about the medical history of Joe's siblings, it didn't leave many to be evaluated. The first criterion is you have to be healthy. Reluctantly, I decided to call my doctor to find out what blood type I was. The first step is to know your blood type. You must be a match in blood. "This is Mrs. Viteri can you please tell me what blood type I am?" The receptionist came back to the phone and said, "You are 0 positive." Tears rolled down my face, you would think I would be excited, but I wasn't! I screamed out, "Why me?"

I was filled with fear of the unknown, fear for my children, myself and my husband. I drove right to work from the hospital. I was exhausted mentally and emotionally but wanted to be at work. A few hours into working a mother called about her child. I am the Director of Smithtown Christian School Early Learning Center. Krista asked about my husband, and I began to cry on the phone as I spoke with her. I'm good at doing that, holding in my emotions and tears until something triggers the pain. She said to me, "Debbie, I want you to know, Kurt, my husband donated his liver to his mother five years ago and is doing well." I couldn't believe what I heard, "Really? He did?" "Yes," and she told me all about it. I asked if he would be open to talking to me, and he did that very day when he picked his child up. I was amazed because I never knew you could even do this surgery.

Another day he even spoke to my daughters and told them of his experience. It seemed to give them a little hope. I thanked him and decided to call the hospital to have an evaluation. Joe's brother Carlos was being evaluated, and the problem was I could not be evaluated until the first person's evaluation was completed. It was very stressful because once the meld score goes up to a twenty-six they will not consider a live donor transplant. By this time, there are more complications on the recipient's life and they also may need a whole liver. This seemed to bring on more stress because we didn't know how fast the meld score elevated. Joe's brother was not able to be a donor; however, we truly appreciated his love and concern to even want to try to save his brother's life.

A living donor has to go through an extensive series of tests which could take a few weeks or even months. During this time of waiting and searching for how the Lord was going to move, there were a few people who wanted to donate which was amazing to me. It was so wonderful to hear how people wanted to help. By this time, I was hoping someone else was going to step up. Even though I knew deep down in my heart, it was going to be me. I was struggling with the idea of being his donor.

However, even though I was afraid, I decided to go for the evaluation when the hospital called. I was supposed to bring someone with me but decided to go alone.

At this time, no family member knew I was considering being a donor.

The day I walked into the hospital on the 14 floor to be evaluated, I was sitting in a chair in the waiting room, thinking things over in my mind. All of a sudden I looked up and there in another part of the waiting room was a familiar face. He was the man I saw at the meeting, the one who came to visit Joe while in the hospital. I said, "Hi there, remember me? I forgot your name." We introduced ourselves again and Vito sat next to me. He asked me why I was there and where Joe was. I explained that Joe was living in New Jersey and that I was there to be evaluated to possibly be a live liver donor. We talked for a while and he gave me a green bracelet that said, "Donate Life"

I'm not the type of person to wear things like that but I did put it on. I figured I guess I'll follow what seems to be going on and I've been wearing it ever since. This was all so new to me, seeing so many sick people who needed some kind of transplant was heart wrenching. Vito then asked if I would like to speak to another woman who also donated her liver to her husband. I said I would love to and he immediately called Maryann. It turned out that this couple lived upstate and were on their way to the hospital for a check-up that very day. They would meet with me about 3:00 p.m. I was excited to meet with them. I thanked Vito and I was called in to meet with the doctors.

When I met with the psychiatrist she went over everything for a psycho evaluation. She explained how the surgery worked, that the new liver may only last for five years in the recipient due to the hepatitis virus infecting the new liver again and the possibilities of death and complications for both of us. Even the possibility of me needing a liver transplant if mine began to fail. I would then be placed on status one before the recipient. They want to make sure the donor is of sound mind and have no psychiatric problems, I passed that test! I told myself, "You are here to gather information, just take it all in, then God will lead and do the rest."

After meeting with her, I met with the nurse practitioner and then the surgeon. When I met Dr. Samstein, he was so gentle and reassuring that everything would go well. He explained that I was his first priority and he answered all of my questions. After that, I went to give blood, they took thirteen vials and then I had an MRI.

By this time, it was about 5 p.m. I was exhausted and a little frustrated that I missed my appointment with the couple I was going to speak with. I had no way of getting in touch with them. I asked the car attendant to please get my van so I could drive home. I was standing outside the hospital waiting for my van when I heard my name called. I looked up and it was Vito, with the couple, Maryann, and Rich. I couldn't believe it. We were introduced, and we went back into the hospital and sat for two hours discussing what to expect to be a live donor. Maryann spoke with me as though she knew me for years; the care and concern she had for me was truly a God sent. She explained every detail and even showed me her scar.

I left the hospital that night knowing the Lord was calling me to lay down my life. How am I going to tell my parents? Another stressful thought! I still had questions but I knew it was no mistake when I thought I opened the wrong door when entering the conference room. God allowed me to meet those men, especially Vito who would be an instrument in my life. He introduced me to people who helped make the turning point in my decision. This decision would not only impact me, my husband and our children but scores of others. This was the biggest decision of my life.

One night my parents were at my home when I sat with them in the living room. I began telling them about the possibility of me being the donor when the phone rang. It was Maryann calling me to see how I was. I explained that I was telling my parents and that she called at the best time. I was able to put her on the speaker phone and both my parents were able to hear her testimony about her experience of being a live donor. She was truly a blessing to both my parents and me. I have to say, my parents were very quiet as they listened and never once did they tell me not to do it. They were both very extremely supportive. A few days later I was together with my parents and brother eating at a restaurant. I had no appetite and for me that is rare. I was feeling overwhelmed, but I have to say, all my immediate family was a great support.

I went to work the next day and told everyone, the Lord was calling me. They knew of my fears and how I was considering running the other way like Jonah did. By now I knew I had to overcome my fears and become obedient to the Lord's will. I explained how He was leading me in such an evident way and I had to be obedient. I have to admit, at this point, I was not so willing; I was exhausted emotionally and physically. It had been a long exhausting journey, by now five years had passed since he was diagnosed. I told the Lord I was not feeling like I could do this, the task was too great! Night after night I went to sleep with this huge task before me. I struggled with the idea that I may die, and that our daughters would be left alone without a father or mother.

I had so many voices around me with such different ideas. When I had a meeting with the pastors I explained I felt like the man hanging from the cliff and when the Lord told him to let go, He would catch him the man looked up and said, "Is there anyone else up there that could help?" I felt like that man, is there anyone else who could help?

In the meantime, Joe was struggling for his life. His lungs constantly had to be drained. He was frustrated, weak in pain and tired, however, his spirit was stronger than ever. My husband loves Jesus so much that his prayer always was and still is "Thank You Lord for what You're doing in our life." Can you believe it? Here is a man who was dying and was thanking God for what He was doing in his life!

I reluctantly agreed with him in a sarcastic attitude, yeah Lord, thanks, thanks a bunch! After my natural man spoke, my heart always shifted to the Spirit man and would say with a humble heart, yes Lord, Thank You. Doesn't the Lord say give thanks in all things? It's not for all things but in all things. He will give you the strength and courage. We were truly walking through the shadow of death, but we feared no evil.

A scripture that carried us during those difficult days were *"The Lord is my shepherd; I shall not be in want. He makes me lie down in green pastures, He leads me beside quiet waters, He restores my soul. He guides me in paths of righteousness for His name's sake. Even though I walk through the valley of the shadow of death, I will fear no evil, for You are with me; Your rod and your staff they comfort me. You prepare a table before me in the presence of mine enemies. You anoint my head with oil; my cup overflows. Surely goodness and love will follow me all the days of my life. And I will dwell in the house of the Lord forever"* (Psalm 23).

One of my favorite devotions from Day by Day during this time was:

Jesus, the Good Shepherd.

My beloved child, I am your Good Shepherd. I have been your Shepherd since the day you were born. I have been guiding you and leading you because I love you. You need never fear that you may have any kind of needs that I will not meet financially, physically, mentally, and spiritually. I am all you need. You will never have to suffer lack in any way. I am your "all in all."

I make a way for you to lie down in green pastures where you can rest and relax. The time to lie down is in the heat of the day. It is in the hard times of life that I prepare a resting place for you and provide cool refreshing waters for you, even the sparkling pure waters that flow down Mt. Hermon. When you are worn and weary with the struggle and the attack of Satan on your life and your spirit, I come and restore your soul. When you drift a little away from the highest dedication and plan for your life, I come to you to restore your soul and I lead you back unto the true path for your feet. There is a spiritual path for you which is your right path. It is the path that I planned for you from before you were born. I will lead you on this path of righteousness.

When death is hovering near you, I am there to protect you from going before your time. And when it is time for you to answer the call, I will take your hand and walk with you through the valley of the shadow of death. You will know no fear in that hour, for I will be with you like I am with you now. My rod will be there to chase away all evil spirits and my staff which I will lend to you, will help you walk a straight road in your old age. I am preparing a delightful table for you. This bounteous supply of the King's dainties in not only reserved for when you cross over. It is yours to enjoy now.

There are many cakes and fruits you have not eaten and many gifts you still have not opened. In front of your enemies, I will give you all these honors, so they will be envious of how much I love you. And as you sit and enjoy the best in the presence of your enemies, I Myself will anoint your head with oil, just like Mary anointed Me. It was an anointing of love that gave Me power to go through the suffering of Calvary. Your cup (your heart) will run over for joy right in the presence of your enemies. Surely goodness and mercy will follow you all the days of your life. Even as the Rock followed the children of Israel in the wilderness (1 Corinthians 10:4), so shall My goodness and mercy follow you and you shall dwell in My presence forever and ever more.

Thank You for lifting our hearts to You. Thank You for carrying us and for being our guide. You are Jehovah-Rohi, Jehovah my Shepherd. "As a shepherd carries his little lambs you will carry me" That's exactly who God is, He is our shepherd.

"He makes us lie down in green pastures; He leads us beside quiet waters" (Psalm 23:2,3).

Question: What fear masters your life?

_____

Ponder: Don't allow fear to control your future.

Scripture: *"I will lie down and sleep in peace, for you alone, O Lord make me dwell in safety" (Psalms 4:8)*

CHAPTER 21

❦

The Peace that Surpasses All Understanding

My Journal: Today is October 10th 2008, our fifteenth wedding anniversary. My parents, the girls and I went to visit Joe in New Jersey. I never imagined visiting my sick husband for our fifteenth anniversary. Instead, we always thought about celebrating in Spain or on a beautiful cruise, however, this is somehow in the plan we never anticipated.

I had to have a sense of humor during this severe emotional trial, so I joked around about instead of giving him a trip for our anniversary I was going to give him half of my liver! Who ever imagined when we stood at the altar 15 years ago; this is what I would be giving as an anniversary gift? God is extremely infinite in His wisdom not to tell us everything up front. We went out for the day, took a horse and buggy ride and went to a special Chinese restaurant with our family members.

The day was beautiful, although, somehow I couldn't believe what was happening in our lives. It just didn't make any sense, and I would not accept this to be the end. I thought about our special wedding day that seemed like

175

it was yesterday. It was so much fun, what a gorgeous day the sky was so blue and majestic. All the pink inpatients were in bloom, it was one of the happiest days of our lives. The Lord always seemed to hear my prayers, He always blessed me with miracle after miracle and now He seemed so distant. I could not comprehend how the Lord gave me the desire of my heart and allowed me to marry such a special man and now it was over. We talked about how the Lord supplied everything miraculously when we were married.

I've always seen God as loving, kind, compassionate, a healer, gentle, and loving in all He does. I struggled with the idea that the Lord allowed me to marry a man who was going to be sick and perhaps die an early death, leaving me as a young widow. God knew Joe would get sick and still He allowed us to fall in love. Then I thought about our wonderful marriage and life together, truth is, we do love each other and that we are perfect for each other in every way.

At night we shared our fears, prayed and talked together. He told me he wasn't forcing me to do anything that I didn't want to and that he would respect my decision. However, he did say to me, if it were you, I would do it for you. Thoughts of running in the other direction entertained my mind at times but I wouldn't allow it to grow and overtake me. I believe in commitment and we take our wedding vows seriously. "For better or for worse, in sickness and in health till death do us part; or what we like to say for all eternity."

True marriage is being a servant to one another. It is not what can I get from that person or what can he/she do for me? True marriage is what can I do for you? It is a ministry. A ministry of love, it's not self-seeking, but it is laying down your life for another, truly becoming one in body, mind, and spirit. It is not 50%-50%. Sometimes your partner can only give thirty percent or ten percent and you have to do the rest. It is totally coming together and helping one another to achieve their goals and yours together. There have been times in our marriage I was not able to give much because I was sick and not feeling well and Joe took care of me.

I understand sometimes this is impossible and there are other options. God does understand and will bless you for your faithful part. The Lord showed Joe before he married me that he was to lay his life down for his wife as Christ laid His life down for His bride. When I heard him say those words to me before we married, it touched my heart deeply and I thought about the prayer I prayed for my husband back in 1988 when I was praying for my spouse. That was one of my requests.

Through fifteen years of marriage, I know how he has laid his life down for me and his family. How? By always putting the Lord first, then his family. That was another request I had, that my husband would be a family man. That he is, in fact, he is everything I prayed for. A co-worker wrote Joe a poem; I'd like to share some of it with you.

(Joe's birth name is Jose, everyone at his job and on all important documents reads Jose, his birth name).
Jose is someone who has great style,
But, it doesn't stop him from giving you a smile.
He is the ultimate family man
It is his priority to be with them when he can.
He will run home at the drop of a hat, It is rare to know a father like that.
Jose is gentle and kind this is a man with an incredible mind.

One day while going through my drawer I found a paper I wrote on August 8, of 1993. I really don't remember who I wrote it to. It sounds like I was preparing a lesson. Whoever it was for, it sure was a lesson for us. God was preparing our hearts way back then. This was two months before we were married. It's funny to see the date because who knew our first daughter would be born on August 9th.

The paper states, "The Word is telling us that God is the center of our home. He is the builder and sustainer of everything in our lives and home. Unless He builds the house, it will fall apart. All of life's securities and blessings are gifts from God rather than from your own achievements. We also see in Psalm 127 that the Lord is telling us that He is the one who provides our shelter, security and food. The Lord also mentions in the Psalms that children are a heritage from the Lord and a reward from Him. Those who fully stay under His shelter and obey Him will find that the Lord will bless them in their coming and going."

Theme: Our marriage and future work in our home. We will build a marriage and a future not as the foolish builder who depends upon his own strength to guide him in the things of this world. Rather we will build our marriage upon the solid Rock, Christ Jesus; who will give us the wisdom, strength, courage and guidance over all of life's trials and tribulations to make our marriage strong to last the time He has ordained it. We believe this foundation is the love of Jesus that will keep our marriage always filled with love, respect and honesty between each other and God Himself. *"Therefore, everyone who hears these words of mine and puts them into practice is like a wise man who built his house on the rock. The rain came down, the streams rose up, and the winds blew and beat against that house; yet it did not fall. The foundation was on the rock"* (Matthew 7:24,25).

I'm not sure who I wrote it for but I know now, it was for this book. I also know God was preparing us way back then for what we were going to encounter. Even when a couple has a strong marriage, you will walk through places you probably have never imagined. Life's journey has a way of doing that! When you both serve the Lord and love each other you can make it through the darkest secret place. You can walk through the valley, it may be a time of asking God to give you a love for your spouse, it may be a time of feeling like you can't go on, but as you spend time with the Lord, and each other, He will renew your strength and your love.

Life Application: Life is made up of joy and sorrow, victory and defeat, success and failure. Sometimes you're on top of the mountain and other times you're in the valley. He will bring you out of the valley so you can walk on top of the mountain. Whether you're in the valley or on the mountaintop of life, always have Christ as your foundation of everything you do and He will enable you to walk in honesty, humility, and respect which will in return fill you with love for each other so you can glorify God in all you do. God is truly awesome; remember dwell in the shelter of the Most High. Even when you're in the valley He is there with you. Then you can face tomorrow with faith instead of fear.

The next weekend, I visited Joe with the girls, I told him all the tests were approved and we were scheduled for November 4th, 2008. We hugged and cried together and blessed the Lord that all was in our favor. That weekend, feeling so sick, with his oxygen tank Joe took me shopping to buy pajamas for both of us. I felt like we were preparing to go on vacation. That's my husband for you, sick, weak, and in pain, he got up and went shopping with our daughters and me, again using his oxygen tank and cane to walk with.

Day Out With Family before Surgery

Going Shopping

When it was time to go home on Sunday Joe asked me to stay one more day. He was feeling sick, he was always in pain, and the pain in his legs was severe. Every minute we all took turns rubbing his legs. I agreed to stay one more night although we had to miss school and work again.

The next morning we said good-bye and we headed out to Route 80. When I reached the road there was a detour sign, I followed the detour and didn't seem to see any more signs.

Leading Of The Holy Spirit

I noticed a man outside raking his leaves, I opened my window and said, "Excuse me, can you please tell me how to get to route 80?" He told me and I thanked him. As I drove away, Bethany noticed he had a green bracelet on. Vito had given me one in the waiting room when I spoke to him that said, "Donate Life." I backed my van up, rolled down my window again and said, "Excuse me, I notice you have a donate life bracelet on. Did someone in your family need a transplant?" He walked over to my car and said, "Yes, my wife needed a liver transplant plant six years ago." I said, really? So does my husband! He asked if I was going to be a live donor and I said, "Yes I was," that I was considering it, that it would be done in about two weeks.

He then explained his wife was afraid for him to be
the donor (which I totally understand) and then she got a
blood infection which she eventually died from. I gave my
sincere condolences to this man, yet I knew what I had
to do. I knew at that point without a shadow of a doubt
the Lord was calling me. I also knew even though I had
fear of the unknown, He would bring me peace. I totally
depended on Him for everything.

CHAPTER 22

***

Total Dependence

For the next few weeks, I felt overwhelmed. Fear would try to control me about my future with my family, feeling exhausted from the day, I would cry myself to sleep at night. When I woke up in the morning, those taunting thoughts were there to plague me one more day, it would not go away. Fear and the unknown were there to stare at me and haunt me one more day.

Lesson #8 God Is Calling Us To Obedience: When God is calling you to do something, it may not always be easy, may not always make sense; may not always be in your time, or even your way. It's not about you; it's about what God wants from you. You must lay down all your dreams and your desires to the point of being obedient to what He wants. Remember, God does want to give us the desires of our heart "If" you seek His Kingdom first, all other things will be added."

He's calling us to obedience; my heart toward the Lord was always one of being used by Him. I constantly asked the Lord to use me, "I'll do whatever You want

184

me to do, I'll go wherever You want me to go, just use me. I desire to be in the center of Your will for my life." I always thought it would be to minister as a missionary in another country to tell someone about the Lord, but never in a million years did I ever know He would be calling me to lay down my life to become a living liver donor. The task seemed too huge.

I thought deeply about Abraham's commitment to the Lord when He asked him to sacrifice Isaac his only son. He was obedient even to the point of death, the death of his son. Not only that but imagine Isaac lying on the altar and waiting for his father to strike him with the knife and being set ablaze by the fire. That was the ultimate test and I don't think I could ever do that!

When you look at what the Lord was really asking, it wasn't to sacrifice his son; it was his obedience God was looking for. "Obedience is better than sacrifice" and when Abraham was obedient even to the point of sacrificing his son, God sent him a ram caught in the thorn bush for him to offer as a burnt offering. God didn't want him to sacrifice his son; He was looking for his obedience. When God saw that Abraham loved Him to the point of sacrificing his son, his only son, he passed the test and was rewarded greatly. *"Against all hope, Abraham in hope believed and so became the father of many nations. Just as it had been said to him, so shall your offspring be"* *(Genesis15:5).*

Obedience is not easy, sometimes we have to suffer. We don't want to suffer, and I know there are many believers who will disagree with this statement. Yes, I know He made a way for us to walk in victory, and I know He wants to prosper us; however, I also know that sometimes, so that we can prosper and walk in victory, we have to walk a road of denial, suffering, and crucifixion. How will we ever know we can walk in victory if we never had defeat? Walking this road is worth everything, although, at the time, we may not see it. I promise you will be able to look back and say, "Now I understand. Thank You, Lord, for helping me never to give up!"

The more I was led by our precious Holy Spirit and became educated at the hospital on the process of being a living donor; fear began to lose its grip on me. I wouldn't say it was totally gone, but it began to fade.

Fear and Misconception

Fear and misconception will try to immobilize and paralyze you until the fear is exposed. Once it is exposed it loses its hold on you. One way I exposed my fear, was by becoming educated on the procedure of becoming a liver donor.

From what was explained to me, and from reading material from UNOS (United Network for Organ Sharing) "Nationwide, the risk of having some type of problem, minor or major after surgery is 15-30%. This includes infection, hernias and swelling (about two in seven cases). Most problems get better on their own; in rare cases, another minor surgery would be needed. In the

United States, there have been two deaths in about 1000 donors." [5]

I never knew the liver would regenerate. What an amazing God and what a miracle! The regeneration occurs rapidly in both patients. Within six-twelve weeks the liver in both recipient and donor will have grown to about 80 percent. Growth then slows down and stops so that at one year the liver is still about 10 percent smaller than its original size. The liver grows to about the size your body needs to function."

Pain management was also a topic of discussion. I have a high tolerance to pain. I've been through surgery three other times, the pain only lasts for a few days, that's not so bad. You do not have to suffer from pain there are plenty of medications to relieve you. After gathering all this information and going through many tests to prepare for surgery I went to a prayer meeting and was prayed over and the Lord filled me with His peace. Even though all seemed to be going well, Satan still tried to keep me from fulfilling my destiny. He wants to stop you from being in the will of God and I know he wanted to stop me!

Fear Spoke To My Soul

One morning while showering a thought crossed my mind, "This is my way of taking you home. I have chosen

[5] Paphlet: <u>Questions and Answers for patients and families about MELD and PELD UNOS</u> Donate Life, Richmand, VA:

this path for you to take in order for you to come home." My heart was gripped with fear and again, I called out the Name of Jesus. I proceeded to say, In the authority of the Lord Jesus Christ, "Satan, you are a liar and the father of lies. I rebuke you in the Name of Jesus; you will not put fear in my heart any longer, I don't buy your lies!"

The Holy Spirit Spoke To My Soul

All of a sudden, a warm and gentle voice within my heart began to speak as the water cascaded on me. "Daughter, do not be afraid, I have called you to this task. I will be with you, do not be afraid. I will send My angels to guard you in all your ways. This will be a testimony for Me, I love you, My daughter, and I will be with you." I blessed the Lord for bringing such peace and affirmation. Fear was broken and joy began to fill my heart.

There may not always be an easy way out of the situation, but the Lord will give you strength to walk through it. The Lord truly is Jehovah Shalom, Jehovah is my Peace. When I came out of the shower I looked for my devotional and again, the Lord confirmed His Word to me.

Devotional: *"He Hath Not Given Me Over To Death."* *Psalm 118:16-24*

No one can die until I give him over to death. I have the keys of life and death. No sickness, no accident, no evil

188

intention of the enemy can take your life. It is virtually impossible for you to die unless I hand you over to death. Even attempted suicides will fail, if I see fit not to hand the individual over to death. Many unnecessarily fear death. Death seems to them to be the conquering foe. But death has its limitations in the life of My righteous saints. It cannot strike while your work is still unfinished. I have a blueprint for your life. As long as you are co-operating in the working out of that blueprint so that your life can declare the works of the Lord, you can rest secure in the knowledge that no one can take your life.

I called My disciples to walk in My footprints. This did not only include suffering and rejection, it also meant triumph over all evil, and the ability to say, "No man taketh it (my life) form Me, I lay it down of Myself."(John 10:18) When you walk in the light, as I am in the light, you have no need to fear an "accidental death." There are no accidents with My righteousness. Neither do you need to fear being cut off before your work is finished. When I call you, you will be ready for the journey home. The Psalmist knew that even the armies of the nations, which had compassed him about, were powerless to take his life until his work on earth was finished. No man can have enough enemies to take his life if I have decreed that he still has a work to do for Me and he is willing to declare My glory.

Many, however, do die before their time, because they are not under this special protection, for they are not doing My perfect will in their lives I, who am perfect love, see this and know if they will continue on this way, they

189

will become further and further away from My plan for their lives. Some will even lose their own souls and go to hell; so I hand them over to death before their time. But not all who die early are cut off because of this. Many who die young already have accomplished all that I intended for them to accomplish. Their work is finished early, for My work of grace has also been completed in their lives. They are now ready for "higher service," and so I call them to their new assignment. Do all My will and rest in Me, knowing that you shall not die, but live and declare the works of the Lord. I have used sickness and dangers to chasten you sore and to draw you closer to Me, but I have not yet handed you over to death. Believe this and walk in victory.

I was also amazed how this devotional used the scripture I always spoke over my husband, "Do all my will and rest in Me, knowing that you shall not die, but live and declare the works of the Lord." Amen! Yes, Lord, I will.

After I read this devotional the peace of Jehovah-Shalom flooded my heart and my mind, it truly was, "The peace that surpasses all understanding." I knew without a shadow of a doubt God was truly calling me to obey Him.

That weekend I drove to New Jersey and told Joe I was going to be his donor; we cried and blessed the Lord that all was working in our favor. Even though we couldn't understand all that God was allowing in our lives, and we couldn't see any reason for it, we still chose to trust Him. At times, we wondered where God was, feeling desperate and deserted, like we were blindfolded and the way ahead of us seemed like a shadow. We truly were walking through the darkest valley. Yet, our hope and light through the valley were, to praise the Lord. All the tests were approved and we made the surgery date for November 4th, 2008.

Be Ready To Declare The Works Of The Lord.

CHAPTER 23

My Sleep Was Truly Sweet

The peace and joy I had, was breathtaking. God gave me
the peace that surpasses all understanding and I had a
new look upon the task before me; I was filled with the
joy of the Lord. The day before surgery Joe came home
with his sisters for the first time in five months. He came
home so that we were able to see a Lawyer and make a
will.

Even though we believed all would go well, we had to
have everything in order, its called wisdom. We asked
his sister Rosa to become the caregiver for our daughters
in case of anything. I couldn't imagine anyone else
raising our girls, but we had to prepare for everything.
Arrangements were made for each daughter and our dog
to be taken care of by friends for the week we were in the
hospital, everything was set. It was another emotional
day, the girls were happy to see their father and he was
happy to be home, even if it was just a few hours.

The Night before Surgery

The night before surgery, I lay in my bed all alone. No husband, children or dog. Most women's dream, everything was silent! I was okay with that, I'm not one to be afraid to be alone, however, my mother wouldn't hear of it. She called me around 7:00 p.m. and asked me to come to her home for the night. I agreed to her request and drove home. As I rested on my bed, I was thinking about where life had brought me, for that night it was like a circle. Here I was sleeping in the house where I grew up with my parents. I slept like I hadn't in months, my sleep was truly sweet.

The next morning, November 4, at 4:30 a.m., I was escorted to the hospital by my brother and parents. I met Joe at New York-Presbyterian Hospital with all of our family. He looked awful; I knew he couldn't take another day. He was bent over in extreme pain from liver failure and the hernia. They gave him a wheelchair to sit in and we all talked. Joe and I gave the hospital permission to film the operation. We were excited to help anyone we could; they would use this film of our liver transplant to teach students. There was a man filming us as we kissed each other to say our good-byes. Saying good-bye to Joe was hard. I believed I would see Joe after surgery. Somehow, even though I knew I would, there was still that small little doubt in my mind what happens if....my liver doesn't fit. Don't forget they took his liver completely out and transplanted mine in.

The attendants called me first, I looked at my immediate family, Joe's family and friends, you could see the look on their faces of desperation, with a mix of fear and joy, like anticipation. I turned around to the camera man as tears began to flow from my eyes as I was being led to the operating room and said, "These are tears of joy."

I was focusing on the joy that was set before us. That we would be a family again!

The minute I entered the room I was greeted by all smiling faces of each attendant. I saw the table in the room and made my way over to lie down. It was truly miraculous, I was not shaking one bit. If you remember, I couldn't stop shaking before my C-section and here I was giving half my liver to my husband, not shaking at all! That was truly miraculous! A living donor has to do everything on their own; you are allowed to change your mind even up to the last minute. They want to make sure you are doing this out of your own free will.

As I laid myself on the table, I thought about Isaac as a living sacrifice. How he had to have laid himself down on the altar, another flash went before my mind about my girls. At this point, I was beginning to get groggy. My arm was stretched out as they sewed a sutcher into my arm, which is a long needle to help them draw blood and out I went.

As one team of doctors was preparing me, in curtain number one was Joe, with his team of surgeons. The Lord blessed us with the exact surgeon I wanted for Joe; Dr. Guarrera, the surgeon I met in the waiting room. I knew he was in good hands. My surgeon was Dr. Samstein which was Maryann's surgeon, so I knew I was in good hands too. Dr. Jean Emond, the head surgeon, who is a pioneer and who had been doing this procedure for the past twenty years went from one side of the room to the other making sure everything went well for Joe and me. The surgery was nine hours for Joe and seven for me.

Immediately after Joe and I were in the operating room, my mother went to the bathroom to cry. She wailed that deep wail, a very painful wail, I know that too well. God again, heard her cry and sent her which she calls, her angel. When she came out of the stall there was a beautiful woman who said to her, "everything is going to be okay, trust God." My mother said, "Yes, I do trust

God, thank you" and she left. From that moment on, my mother felt comforted. She also had two very close friends, Alice, and Millie, waiting with her, along with everyone else.

The clock ticked very slowly while everyone waited patiently. Each of our parents, siblings and friends waited until one of the surgeons came out to speak with them. About nine hours later, the doctor came out and said, "All went well." He said, "As soon as they connected everything, the bile began to flow beautifully, that my liver was a great motor." He also said, "Our arteries and veins fit so well it was as if we were twins." Not only did I have to be a blood match, but a tissue match as well. Just to think, we matched in everything. It was as though we were related. The doctors said, "They could not get over how well we connected." Sometimes, during surgery, the veins tear and it's impossible to perform the connection. Mine were so healthy, they fit like a glove. They were also able to fix the hernia that was strangling him.

It's amazing to hear the doctors referring to us as twins, here's a man, born in Ecuador and a woman, from Smithtown, Long Island, fitting together like twins. Both of Joe's parents were born and raised in Ecuador when their families emigrated from Spain (mother) and Italy (father) during world war one. Joe's mom was fifteen when she met her husband; it's very common in those countries to marry young. She had eight children by the time she was twenty-six years old.

Viteri Family in Ecuador

Joe's parents wanted to give their children the ability to improve their life, so my father-in- law wrote a letter to President Johnson asking permission for his family to settle down in America. President Johnson welcomed everyone, so his parents began to prepare for the move. Joe's oldest brother lived with his grandfather, He and two siblings lived with their uncle, and Joe's twin sisters lived with their aunt in a convent. The two youngest siblings went with their parents for two years so that they could find work, buy a home and then call for their children. At the age of nine and a half, Joe remembers going on the large airplane and meeting his parents at the airport to begin a new life in America. Who knew years later, Joe would marry me, a girl from Long Island who would be used to save his life. Only God!

The next day I woke up, saw my mother and asked her to call the girls. She reassured me she had already done that. I asked how everything went and was told all went well. Joe and I were recovering right next to each other between curtains. My brother asked me if I wanted to see Joe and I agreed to be placed in a wheelchair. I was strolled over to see him hooked up to all kinds of machines. I didn't remember any of this but when I saw the pictures it brought back my memory and I'm so happy to have them.

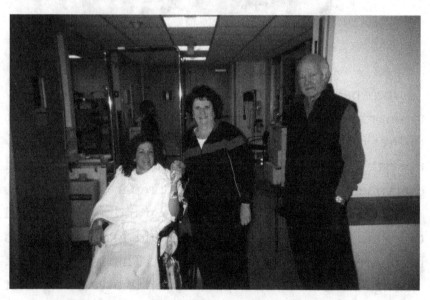

My Parents and I Day after Surgery.

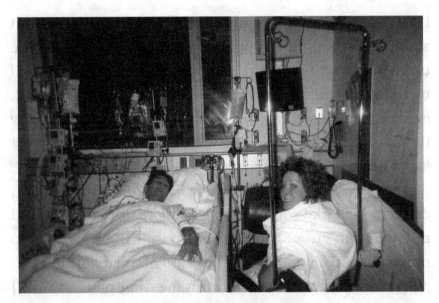

Day after Surgery

After one day, I was moved to the seventh floor to continue my recovery; right in front of the nurse's station. Joe continued to stay where he was. By day number two I had to get up and walk to the bathroom. Bent over and hobbling, I made it, I felt as though I was torn in half. Day three, my parents and daughters came to visit. I felt so bad because I was very sick that day. I tried to eat a little soup my mother-in-law brought, and it did not agree with me. The soup was delicious but I wasn't ready to eat. Every smell made me feel like vomiting, in fact, that's just what I was doing when my girls came.

I felt so bad, I heard Jessica say, "I want to go home, please take me home." As I was getting sick I was yelling "Go, take her home." Of course, they didn't want to leave me and waited until I began feeling a little better. I think

I had a bad reaction because I was pressing the med unit so much. I thought the pain I would feel was going to be unbearable so I tried to prevent that by giving myself meds. Even taking the Oxycodone made me feel sick, every time I closed my eyes I began to hallucinate. I saw flowers opening and closing with bright colors. It almost looked like I was looking through a kaleidoscope.

I was resting on an inflatable bed and every time it deflated I felt like someone was going to grab my feet and pull me from out of bed. I was also wearing leg wraps to prevent blood clots. I decided to stop all medications and just take Tylenol and rely on my heating pad. I think I was in that particular room about four days.

I managed to get out of bed a few times to walk down the hall to see Joe. There he was in bed, eating chicken and rice and beans. It was pretty funny, I was sick to my stomach and he was up and eating. The feeling I had was very similar to being pregnant, smells bothered me and I felt nauseous. Joe didn't have a roommate, so I helped myself to the empty bed until I was asked to leave. It was so nice to see him feeling good enough to eat, I was really happy for him. The doctors told me this would happen, role reversal. He was so sick so he felt like a million dollars; I was already healthy so I felt like a million dollars in counterfeit bills.

When my mother visited me, she said, "this experience has been "tears of joy" and I said, "Yes mom, "painful", tears of joy." Then it hit me, that should be the title of my book. Don't forget, I had been writing about my journey since 2003. When Joe was first diagnosed I wrote for my own therapy.

After I was home, I changed the title to my book and lost the whole thing! I'm not computer literate and didn't save my work on any file. I have learned since then! This difficulty was not going to defeat me! I found a few pages hand written and started all over again. Thank You, Jesus, for helping me!

It would be nice if the title was something funny or eye-catching, but this is truly what we have experienced. "Painful, Tears of Joy." This whole journey has been emotionally, spiritually and physically painful, with lots of tears; however, God can turn your tears into tears of joy.

The Bible declares, *"Weeping may endure for the night, but joy comes in the morning" (Psalm 30:5).*

After four days I was moved to another room down the hall from Joe. They don't like to put family in the same room it can cause mix up between medications and they also want their patient to walk. Every day I would walk to my husband's room and lay next to him in bed. It was a treat when we had potato chips at night. He enjoyed them so much; he had been on a no salt diet for one year because a high level of sodium increases the amount of water retention in the body. This can make ascites (belly) and edema (leg) swelling worse. So these potato chips were a real treat. The small things we take for granted.

I think I wore maybe two sets of the pajamas I bought and he didn't wear any except that gown with the wide opening. We ate our chips and laughed at my desire to have matching pajamas and said, "What was I thinking!" Even in the hospital we made the most of it and had fun.

Every day we both made progress and took our daily strolls around the nurse's station to admire our beautiful flowers people bought us. We were not allowed to keep them in our room. By this time, I saw my husband's color change, Before surgery, the color of his skin was black, he is olive tone, and now a few days after surgery he had pink cheeks.

Our Daily Walks.

As time went on, Joe became strong enough after all the tubes were taken out of him to be able to meet me in my room. He and the girls surprised me one day when they came to visit with me. It was so precious when I saw them all walking in my room to make sure I was feeling comfortable.

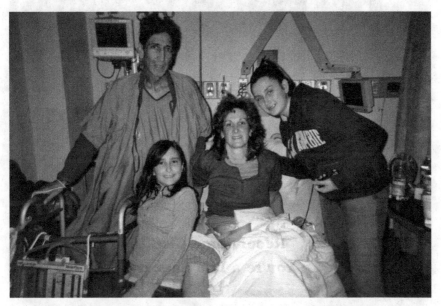

Surprise...My Family Came to Visit Me

When Joe had his tube removed I was with him in his room. In walked an intern and asked me to move over to the other side of the room. He told Joe to take a deep breath and when he did, the intern grabbed the tube and pulled about 40 inches of the tube out of Joe's body. It whipped across the bed; I couldn't believe that tube was inside his body. The tube was kept inside of him after surgery to help drain the fluids.

A few days after surgery the hospital staff gave me a cute teddy bear that wore a life preserver that said, "You're a Life Saver." I'll always cherish it.

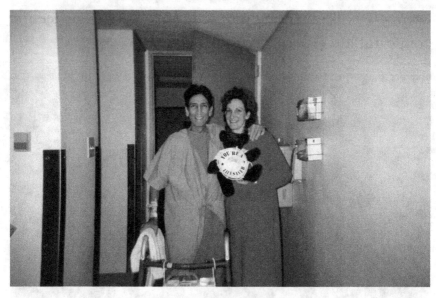

Receiving a Gift
You're a Life Saver

CHAPTER 24

Surrender

I was very happy all went well, but still had a sore spot in my heart because I was so expecting a supernatural miracle. We really believed we could have woken up and the doctors could have said, "We have no explanation but"...As I laid in bed with this deep concern in my heart, I turned on the TV and found a wonderful Christian station TBN, I never knew about it. It was so uplifting and encouraging. A few minutes into listening Pastor Benny Hinn came on TV and he told a story about a pastor's wife who had cancer. He continued to say how if she took the medications she could possibly be alive today. This story was amazing to me because we all know Pastor Benny is used by God in the healing ministry; and when he told this story it really ministered to me. This is a personal conviction and I want to extend my sincere condolence to this family; however, the Lord used this story to encourage me.

Once again, I said, "okay, Lord." Even after the surgery I still had to come to terms with "let Your will be done, not mine." I know the Lord could have healed in a different way but He chose this way. The key is,

I Had To Learn To Surrender To The Will Of God.

It's not easy, especially because I wanted to use this opportunity to witness the miraculous. The important thing to remember is that God's will is always the best way for us. We have two choices to take, either forget God's will and go our own way, which will bring a mess, or forget our own will and follow God. This will bring blessings.

The day came when Joe was able to go home. After ten days he walked out wearing his leather coat. I was happy for him, I truly was, but somehow, it wasn't supposed to happen this way. I was left alone in the hospital for another two days. My stay should have only been five days and twelve days later I left. My white cell count was slightly high and they wanted to make sure I was clear of any infection. If an infection sets in it could be life threatening. So I really was extremely happy and grateful my doctor was being extra cautious. I decided to try to enjoy my last two days alone. I sat in the TV room with patients and families and encouraged them about their recovery, and was able to share my story.

I have to say again, the care we received at New York-Presbyterian Hospital was remarkable. Everyone truly took such great care of us. The day came when I was released and I went to Rosa's house where Joe was living. I cannot explain the feeling I had when we hugged and snuggled in bed together. He was no longer in desperate pain; it was now a pain we both shared, one of recovery. We helped each other with everything we needed.

After two days I said good-bye again and left for home. Joe's sister, Maria, my mother and Debbie, my friend, were my caregivers. Maria staycd with me for a week along with my mother and Debbie came over to keep me company when Maria left and mom had to go out. I will never forget the arrival home; my girls and their friends came running out to greet me. We were so excited to see each other and to begin our life. When I came home I heard so many people refer to this event as a miracle. I had to put everything into perspective and say with a humble heart yes Lord, it is a miracle.

There was a saying I learned at Christ For The Nations which says

"The Miracles Of God Are In The Deep Waters Of Obedience."

Joe came home for good the day before Thanksgiving; it was truly a thankful day. We had much to give thanks for, and we were, with a grateful heart. There was so much love and excitement in the air which overflowed with showers of blessings in such generous ways from family and friends. As I looked around the room there were gorgeous flowers, baskets of food, and cards from all our family and friends. He was still so frail but every day he got stronger and stronger.

Six weeks after re-cooperating we were invited to speak at New York-Presbyterian's 1000 transplant celebration. We were 1017 and they asked Joe and me to share our experience. It was an honor and so marvelous to see all the recipients and donor families. They all welcomed us and after the celebration, we were interviewed by ABC News.

Our interview was aired that very night. I wanted to share so much but had little time. They really focused on our fears. We had so many fears to overcome and with the help of the Lord and the liver team at the hospital, we were able to do just that! The clip also showed me in the operating room and my liver in a bag being carried to the next room for transplant.

They gave details on how the liver regenerates between six to twelve weeks and how being a donor is very crucial in helping to save lives because 19 people die daily waiting for a liver transplant in New York alone and that statistic will increase yearly. We hope and pray that small clip had an impact on the nation. You can be used to give the gift of life. We were also asked to write an article for NYPH paper, I would like to share it with you.

Article From My Husband, The Recipient

I was diagnosed with hepatitis C and stage four fibrosis of the liver in early 2003. I am a 54-year-old, Spanish male who contracted the disease after receiving three blood transfusions in the early year of 1982 after a car accident. I managed to live five years asymptomatic by receiving herbal treatments and taking care of my liver by living a healthy lifestyle that sustained the organ for 33 years. However, eventually, the illness progressed to total deterioration and liver failure that nearly caused my death.

In May 2008, I was informed by a friend to seek treatment at New York-Presbyterian/Columbia. One month later, I suffered an encephalopathy attack and was admitted to the hospital in a comatose state and was treated by a professional team of liver specialists. The doctors in the emergency room worked for hours to revive me and, upon breathing on my own, were moved to the intensive care unit for one week and spent one month in the hospital. Three days after regaining consciousness, I was informed by my family that I was being treated at one of the best medical facilities in New York City and by a staff of medical professionals who are caring and committed to saving my life by attempting everything possible.

During this time, my body wasted to a weight of 118 pounds and I was unable to walk from being confined to the hospital bed for one month and had to learn to walk again. I was also suffering from extensive body pain, fatigue, loss of hair, numerous thoracenteses and paracenteses. I was also compromised with breathing problems due to an upper respiratory infection promoted by extensive fluid accumulation outside the right lung that eventually collapsed from the illness. The medical team went to work immediately to complete an extensive liver transplant evaluation in one month to be placed on the list for eligibility to receive a liver. Despite making the eligibility list, I was advised that due to my MELD score dropping from 22 to 16 that the only alternative left was to obtain a living liver donor from a family member.

As a liver recipient, I waited two months for a living donor and was unable to obtain a liver through a healthy person despite having seven siblings; five brothers and twin sisters due to medical complications. During these difficult times, between my faith and my parents and siblings devoting their lives to nurse me back to good health to be able to endure the liver transplant operation, I resided in New Jersey with my sister Rose. Debbie's family and our church congregation were also a great supporting factor in assisting my family with every emotional and financial need that gave me the psychological stability to focus on staying alive until a donor was found. Eventually, the miracle living donor became my wife (Debbie).

It is important to acknowledge that God orchestrated this plan and provided the best team of surgeons. I am also extremely grateful to all the staff at New York Presbyterian Hospital for their empathy, dedication, and care for the safety of their patients. My deepest and sincere gratitude goes to the professionalism and commitment of Dr. Jean Emond, Dr. Guarrera, and Dr.Samstein for the surgery and all the medical staff who were an important and instrumental part in my living liver donor transplant operation and recovery.

This testimony would be incomplete without thanking God and giving my precious Debbie the credit for the gift of life as a liver organ donor despite the risks to her life and the lives of our young daughters, Bethany, and Jessica. The greatest, most selfless act is to give life to another person by denying yourself through organ donation so that another individual may benefit by obtaining the gift of life. Will you donate today? A sincerely grateful recipient of the gift of life, Jose

Article From The Donor

My husband and I are living proof that a living liver donation is a miracle and a gift from God. In 2003, my husband was diagnosed with hepatitis C, stage four fibrosis. After battling this illness for many years with different forms of remedies, Joe's illness progressed. A friend told me about NYPH and the special liver unit they have. I felt impressed to change doctors immediately. I am so happy I did because a few months after making the change I had to rush my husband to the emergency room with encephalopathy. We arrived at NYPH's emergency room July 27, 2008; the professional team knew exactly how to remove the poison from his body. After stabilizing him, they moved him to a new unit where he was given over to the liver specialist team. His diagnosis was end- stage liver disease.

He was evaluated to receive a liver from the list; however, due to the fact of a low meld score, his chances of receiving a liver from the list were slim. During his stay in the hospital, I learned about living liver donation. I never heard of it and was fearful to even consider the idea; even though I was fearful, I needed to educate myself. I made an appointment to speak with the living liver donation team and they educated me with such care and support. The day I met my surgeon, Dr. Samstein, I was nervous and concerned especially since I am a mother of two children. He explained everything in a detailed manner and his gentle ways made me feel safe knowing I was his priority. I also met a woman who donated to her husband a few months ago as well as other transplant recipients.

What helped me make the biggest decision of my life was the support of the liver team, others who have gone through the procedure and my family and friends. I know there were thousands of prayers sent to the Lord on our behalf, and for this, I am forever grateful. My immediate family, mother, father, and brother, never once discouraged me; they stood by my side with such strength and love. It is four weeks since our surgery and as I reminisce, your smiling faces are engraved in my mind. 7HS, my husband and I are grateful for your impeccable care and service to us.

This has truly been what I call "Painful Tears of Joy" The joy far outweighs the pain, when I see my husband doing so well, full of energy and doing things he hasn't been able to do in years, it brings such joy to my heart. Our girls have their father back and I have my husband back. This opportunity to give life to another has enriched me forever. I can now look forward to many years as a family. He is home for the Holidays; we give thanks from the bottom of our hearts. If you know someone who needs a liver, please take the opportunity to give life; you will never regret it. With Gratitude, Debra

I am humbled to think of how the Lord used me to give my husband life. It is so important to donate living or deceased organs, too many people are waiting. Not only are they waiting for livers, but other organs as well. I met so many wonderful people who are dying unnecessarily. Consider being a live donor, the discomfort I went through varies from individuals and mine truly was nothing. When I think of the small price of giving half of my liver to save my husband from dying an early death, I am overjoyed by the life my husband has and the goodness of the Lord. Organ Donation is truly the gift of life, Thank You Lord for using me!

CHAPTER 25

He Is Jehovah Rapha

We were blessed with a trip to Florida, eight weeks after the transplant, by Joe's sister, Maria and her husband Allan. The doctors didn't want us traveling so soon, but we had to get away. First, we celebrated Christmas with our family and then packed our bags to head for Miami; to my sister and brother-in-laws condo for New Year's, 2009. Joe's body had to get used to the rejection medication, so at times, he was quite sick from being poisoned from too much medication. He had to go to the nearest lab to get blood work to keep watch over his numbers. His medication had to be lowered due to over medicating. Sometimes that happens until the doctor's figure out how much your body needs. Not to worry, they keep a close watch on you. Even though Joe and I were recuperating, the girls had so much fun using the pool, walking on the beach and enjoying some parks. It was so much fun bringing in the New Year together and giving God praise for what He had done.

Florida Eight Weeks after Transplant

My Journal: Today, January 8, 2009, a few weeks after the trip to Florida. I'm doing well, went back to work after eight weeks. I'm noticing I have to nap when I get home; my energy level has dropped, but it will change after a while. As for Joe, he's doing well, his body is getting used to the new organ, including two rejection medications.

He's going back to work in a few days, he's just amazing! We did have to close Living Proof Counseling Services. Maybe one day we will open again, time will tell. Fifteen years ago, The Lord gave me the name Living Proof Counseling Services for our counseling practice. I love that name because both Joe and I are Living Proof to God's faithfulness, and now we are living proof that living liver donation saves lives.

In March 2009, four months after surgery, Pastor Gary Zarlengo asked Joe and I to share our testimony in church. After we spoke, he preached a dynamic service on "God will make a way where there seems to be no way." He gave scriptural examples from the Bible on how God heals in different ways; once again, I was in awe of how God did make a way where it seemed impossible.

Speaking at Church

After service, there was a woman who approached me as I was walking in the parking lot to get to my car. She explained that the Lord healed her while on the operating table and she didn't have to have her gall bladder removed. God helped me to receive that graciously and said, "Praise the Lord, I'm happy for you." Joe and I believed for that too, but He chose to take our gallbladder out. God does have a sense of humor! You see, when you are a liver donor you must have your gall bladder removed too. They can remove the gall bladder without removing the liver, but they cannot remove the liver without removing the gall bladder. Same goes for the recipient. Since the liver is replaced with a new one, the gallbladder has to be removed.

Lesson #9 The Lord Heals Some People Supernaturally and Others Naturally:

We will never understand why The Lord heals some people supernaturally and others naturally. We believed for our supernatural miracle up to the very end. We were imagining waking up from surgery and hearing "we didn't have to remove Joe's liver and yours because" . . . . I don't know why he was never healed supernaturally; one thing I do know is that this experience has taught us things we could have never learned with a supernatural healing. One way or another, it does not change the fact that He is, Jehovah- Rapha, the Lord who heals (Exodus 15: 25, 26).

A. The Jehovah Who Healed In The Bible Is The Same Jehovah Who Heals Today:

The name Jehovah Rapha means Jehovah heals. I have learned many years ago that the word Rapha means to restore, to heal, to cure or a physician.

I know that God is concerned about your physical wellbeing, but I believe, He's more concerned about your spiritual well-being. You can get to Heaven if your body is wrecked with pain and sickness if your spirit is right with God, and you will have a glorified body and be renewed. However, if your body is healthy and your spirit is sick and full of sin, you will not make Heaven and your body will see decay. He does want us whole on earth; however, Heaven is our ultimate goal.

In April, five months after the transplant, we were on another jet with Rosa and Steve headed to Aruba. Both trips were a miracle, we were a family again! I have to say Aruba was gorgeous! Every morning I got up at 5:00 a.m. to make sure we got our bamboo umbrella at the beach. While standing in line, I heard what sounded like birds of paradise. There were hundreds of birds singing their beautiful songs. As I watched our girls on the jet ski with their uncle having fun, it was so rewarding and sobering to me at the same time. Only five months ago, we were facing the battle of our life, and now, here we were, in Aruba. This vacation was very sobering because I thanked the Lord for helping me to make the right decision. Joe and I had a wonderful time together with Rosa, Steve, and our children. Every day, Joe and I thanked the Lord for His faithfulness and cherished each moment. Joe had to be careful about doing any extra activity because he was really quite frail.

Aruba Five Months after Transplant

One month after we returned from Aruba, which was May 2009, Joe had his first biopsy which looked good. This was six months after surgery.

One of my favorite scriptures that I continued to read during this time was Psalm 91. I love this scripture because I felt like I was living through it.

Bible Application: *"He who dwells in the shelter of the Most High will rest in the shadow of the Almighty. I will say of the Lord. "He is my refuge: and my fortress, my God in whom I trust." Surely He will save you from the fowler's snare, and from the deadly pestilence. He will cover you with His feathers and under His wings you will find refuge; His faithfulness will be your shield and rampart. You will not fear the terror of night, nor the arrow that flies by the day, nor the pestilence that stalks in* *the darkness, nor the plague that destroys at midday. A thousand may fall at your side, ten thousand at your right hand, but it will not come near you. You will only observe with your eyes and see the punishment of the wicked. If you make the Most High your dwelling even the Lord who is my refuge then no harm will befall you; no disaster will come near your tent. For He will command His angels concerning you to guard you in all your ways. They will lift you up in their hands so that you will not strike your foot against a stone. You will tread upon the lion and the cobra. You will trample the great lion and the serpent. Because he loves me, says the Lord, I will rescue him: I will protect him for he acknowledges my name. He will call upon me and I will answer him I will be with him in trouble. I will deliver him and honor him. With long life will I satisfy him and show him my salvation" (Psalm 91).*

B. **Love God:** The key here is to, love God. "Because He loves me," then His promises follow, I will **rescue** him, I will **protect** him, I will **answer** him, I will **deliver** him, I will **satisfy** him **with long life.** This is what we stood on and believed for.

Take a moment and meditate on this promise.

CHAPTER 26

Heaven Bound

In September 2009, Joe, the girls and I picked up our precious Uncle Frank and took him apple picking. I will never forget that gorgeous day when we picked him up. He was not expecting us, but when we arrived at his home and told him we were taking him apple picking, he put on his coat and hat with so much enthusiasm and slowly walked to the car with a huge grin on his face. He enjoyed watching all of us pick apples; the day was so gorgeous

Great Uncle Frank

My Journal: Today was a beautiful day, October 10, 2009. I am grateful for another year. The Lord is faithful to allow us to celebrate our sixteenth anniversary. When I look back to our fifteenth anniversary which was only one year ago, I didn't know if it was going to be our last and final celebration. Our marriage has sure been tested to the max; I know it is built on solid rock.

We took our daughters, parents, and uncle and went to the Marriott overnight. The girls love using their pool and we always have so much fun. It's only five minutes from home, and we feel like we're on vacation. Little do my parents know we planned a surprise 50th wedding anniversary party at the East Wind Hotel for next week.

Mom and dad will be so surprised especially to see all their friends along with her brother and sister from Texas. Thank God for my husband who encouraged me to give them a party. After talking to my brother, who agreed, we began making plans.

It's only been ten months since surgery and we almost didn't put one together. Thank God Joe and I talked and agreed that mom and dad should most definitely have a 50th party. After everything we went through, it is amazing we can celebrate.

Heaven Bound!

You never know from month to month what life is going to bring. Who knew three months after apple picking and the beautiful party, on December 27th we would be weeping as our precious uncle was laid to "rest," or should I really say, he went home for the holidays? Somehow I cannot picture him resting. He's in our home, Heaven. His journey of life here on earth is over and his new life in Heaven has just begun.

A picture the Lord placed in my mind when I was describing his homecoming to my daughters was this. He was ninety-one and you know what a ninety-one man who has been suffering from congestive heart failure looks like? I don't need to say anymore, however, in my vision he looks like he's thirty-three.

Only one week ago, he, my mother and I were discussing what Heaven would be like. Frank wondered if he would remain ninety-one. My thought was that he would be thirty-three, the age Jesus was when He ascended to Heaven. He liked that idea, I picture him strong, no wrinkles, brown hair, like he looked when he was thirty-three; wearing the white robe of righteousness. He is walking down a long aisle of angels blowing their trumpets, but he's not alone. He is being escorted by our precious Lord and Savior, Jesus. When they walk to the end of the aisle he approaches God Almighty sitting on His throne.

The Father says in a strong yet gentle tone of voice "Hello Frank before I let you into My Kingdom, let Me just take a moment and open My Book (The Lambs Book of Life) to make sure your name is written down."

He slowly opens the Book and scrolls through thousands upon thousands of names and in just an instance; He sees his name clearly written: Mr. Frank Gatti. God the Father looks up toward Frank and says with a smile "Welcome into My Kingdom, My good and faithful servant."

The gates open wide and Frank approaches the Kingdom of eternity. As Frank begins to make his way, he hears on a loud speaker, "Will Jessie and Jenny Gatti and all other family members come to the main entrance, there has been an arrival." His family runs to the gate and sees Frank. There is so much excitement! His family cannot wait to show him around his new home. He's greeted with hugs and kisses by his mother, wife, siblings and his precious sister-in-law, Julie.

His brother Joe says, "Frank wait until you see the river of life, it's around the corner." Dominick says, "Yes and the streets are of pure gold." Mary and Jim come running and wrap their arms around him, there is so much joy. As they begin to approach the corner trying to make it to the river of life they begin to hear Heavenly praises to God the Father, and to Jesus, God the Son, "To Him who sits on the throne and unto the Lamb, to Him who sits on the throne and unto the Lamb, be blessings and glory and honor and power forever.

Take a moment and sing this to the Lord a few times, you will have a visitation from the Holy Spirit.

Can you imagine this vision? If you have lost a family member or friend, picture them in this beautiful place. Remember, the Bible declares you go from death to life. The sting of death has been broken. *"Where O death is your victory? "Where O death is your sting? But thanks be*

to God who gives us the victory through Christ our King"
(1 Corinthians 15:55).

If you think of it this way it will make it a little easier
for you to let go. Keep your mind Heaven bound that is
always how my uncle signed our cards, Love your Heaven
bound Uncle Frank. We miss him dearly, but I do have a
grateful heart that my husband didn't go first.

*"Then the angel showed me the river of the water of
life, as a clear as a crystal, flowing from the throne of God
and of the Lamb down the middle of the great street of the
city. On each side of the river stood the tree of life, bearing
twelve crops of fruit, yielding its fruit every month. And
its leaves of the tree are for the healing of the nations. No
longer will there be any curse. The throne of God and of
the Lamb will be the city, and his servants will serve him.
There will be no more night. They will not need light of
a lamp or the light of the sun, for the lamb, God will give
the light, and they will reign for ever and ever" (Revelation
22:1-5).*

CHAPTER 27

From Faith to Faith and Victory to Victory!

Another year has passed, it is November 4, 2010; we celebrated our two year "Liversary" today. Joe had his second biopsy fifteen months after surgery in April, and it came back that his liver was back in stage 2-3!! Stage 2 is inflammation and early fibrosis in one part of the liver. Stage 3 is the liver having moderate to severe fibrosis.

Our reaction was, "Wow that was fast! Okay Lord, now what are You trying to teach us?" We were not desperate or heartbroken; although, I did cry and feel sick to my stomach for a few days. Just the thought of seeing him, our daughters, or me go through that agonizing pain again was overwhelming! However, this time, there was a difference.

Lesson #10 Stronger Faith: We were stronger in our faith and trust because we had experienced the provision of the Lord. Our level of maturity and confidence was greater.

Bible Application: As I went through this experience, I thought about the story of Moses. It shows the Lord's provision when tragedy strikes and how Moses' mother walked by faith for the life of her child, just like, I have been walking by faith for the life of my husband.

By faith, Moses' mother hid him for three months and placed him in a basket. His sister then sent him down the Nile River to set him free from the Egyptians who wanted to kill the firstborn. His mother truly had faith and God honored her by allowing the Princess of Egypt to find her son and raise him as her own.

Moses' mother had no idea her son was going to be used as an instrument of God to rescue her, her family and the Israelites out of slavery. She was walking by faith and did everything she could to save her son. He was not an ordinary child, God, had a bigger plan and purpose for his life.

A. God Has A Bigger Plan and Purpose For Your Life and Mine!

Years later, after Moses found out he was Hebrew; he left Egypt and all its glory. While tending sheep, Moses noticed a bush on fire, yet, it didn't burn up. It was very common to see a bush on fire in the desert because it is so dry. This one, however, was different and when he walked over to see it, the voice of God spoke to him and said, "Moses, Moses" and Moses replied, "Here I am," God said to him, "I am the God of Abraham, Isaac and Jacob." God wanted to let Moses know He heard the cry of His people. God told Moses, *"I have seen the misery of my people, I have heard them crying out, and I am concerned with their suffering" (Exodus 3:7).*

God gave instruction to Moses through the burning bush to rescue the Israelites from bondage. Moses asked God; "Suppose I go to the Israelites and say to them, "The God of your fathers has sent me to you, and they ask me, "What is His name? Then what shall I tell them?" God said to Moses, "I AM, WHO I AM." The Lord gave himself this personal name; a Hebrew phrase that indicates action. God was saying, "I wish to be known as the God who is present and active." It expresses His faithful love and care and His desire to live in fellowship with you.

B. God Sees You and Is Concerned With Your Suffering:
The God who lives in Heaven can reach down and hear us; He is concerned with your suffering and mine. He wants you to know, "I Am your strength", "I AM your peace", "I AM your healer", and I AM everything!" "Whatever you need Me to be today for your situation, I AM."

C. Our Job Is To Trust and Obey and Know He Will Be With You To The Very End:

God reveals Himself to His covenant people, as the unchanging God who remains faithful to His Word through many generations. When I heard Joe's liver was back in stage 2-3 I felt like the wandering Israelites who Moses brought out of Egypt. They went around the same desert for forty years looking for the promise land. I felt like the Israelites because, Joe was diagnosed seven years ago, April 2003 and here we are seven years later April 2010. I began to sing that silly song, "She's been going around the mountain when she comes," . . . Lord, we don't have to go around the mountain like the Israelites; I don't believe we're going around the same mountain because the Lord is still trying to teach us something we missed the first time. We're not perfect; however, I know we learned our lesson well. God doesn't promise your life would be filled with only wonderful days, or that you wouldn't go through a drought.

Lesson #11 We Will Go, From Faith To Faith, From Victory To Victory and From Glory To Glory:

A. **How Will We Go From Faith To Faith If We Don't Have Anything To Believe For?**
B. **Each Trial Is A New Lesson to Be Learned**: What's the key? If we are willing!

Instead of putting our heads down and feeling like we missed God or getting angry with Him, we chose to focus our hearts and minds on God and His Word and never entertained any of those negative thoughts. I did not want to allow a root of bitterness to overtake my soul. A root of bitterness is an intense attitude of the heart that has hatred and resentment toward God or others. Instead of allowing our hearts to go in that direction, we continued to hold our banner high by proclaiming and declaring God rules and reigns. Jehovah is our banner,

Jehovah-Nissi (Exodus 17:15). God is in control! Joe and I will continue to raise our banner and declare the victory.

While attending Bible School I learned that "A raised banner during the time of the Israelites declared God's victory that victory was always won no matter what the odds." You can learn so many precious lessons from the wandering Israelites.

C. **Don't Forget What God Has Done For You**: Even after God revealed Himself to the Israelites in so many ways they still **grumbled and complained.** They doubted God, they forgot the parting of the Red Sea, the healing of the bitter waters, and forgot the manner from Heaven so they could eat. They questioned God's goodness and even His presence.

**I Will Never Forget All The Miracles
God Has Done For Me!**

D. **God Still Performed Miracles:** The Israelites put God to the test and rebelled against the Most High; read Psalm 78. It says "Is the Lord among us or not?" Even after they questioned God, in His mercy, He caused water to spring from a rock to quench their thirst. "Moses smites the rock with his rod and water came gushing out." Can you imagine water coming out of a rock? Talk about a supernatural miracle!

God gave Moses the rod to perform His miracles. God's power, which was the power of the Holy Spirit, worked through the rod through the hands of Moses. Imagine the day Moses was leading the Israelites out of Egypt. It was a day of victory until they came to the huge body of water. It appeared like there was no way out of the situation. The enemy was behind them, the chariots of Pharaoh and the huge sea was in front of them. Do you ever feel like that? Like you're being covered and consumed in your trial? There is no way out! I'm going to drown! What does Moses do? Quit? And say this trial is too big? No, He exercises his faith and lifts the rod in front of the sea and God parts the waters for everyone to walk through. The rod that Moses carried was a symbol of God's great power.

Another example of a battle won is when Moses and his tribe were fighting against the Amalekites. Whenever Moses raised his hands the enemy was defeated. We have God's power today! Lift your hands to God in prayer, and watch the enemy be defeated! What enemy is fighting against you?

When Moses was tired and could no longer hold his arms up, Aron and Hur were right beside him to hold his hands high and the battle was won. Moses then built an altar and called it "The Lord is my banner." "It is this rod, as the banner of God, which brought the victory" (Exodus 17).

In the same way, when Joe and I could no longer pray and raise our hands to God, the body of Christ held us up and continued to believe for our miracle. With Jehovah Jesus on our side, who is our Banner, **We can go from strength to strength and from victory**

231

to victory. You have read about all my miracles: I will never stop trusting God.

"For this is the victory that overcomes the world, even our faith" (1 John 5:4).

Devotional: *"The Valley of Sorrows is the Place of Blessings"* (Psalm 84:5)

Your strength is in Me, you have no strength. I am your strength. I have unlimited strength. My strength endures forever and under all conditions. So My child, if your strength is in Me, what do you have to fear? Your heart is my dwelling place, for in it is the Highway that leads you to Zion. It has that beautiful shining light that reaches far out into the most remote areas of darkness and sadness. When your heart has a Highway to Zion, you will never fear any valley experience; for no matter how deep your valley may be, your heart has within it the glory Highway that leads right through to Zion even the eternal abode of glory. It is here that My glory rests from it there are sent out glory beams of light that pierce through the darkness and from the gloom straight into your heart. That is why in your heart, is the Highway to Zion. Follow that glory light and it will take you home to glory and you will daily be in Holy Communion with me on the glory wavelength of communion.

Every painful experience, every valley of "Baca" (which means sorrow and suffering) will become a valley of blessings. It will cause your soul to receive a great supply of the early rain, even before others receive it, and your dry places, even the mud holes in your life, will fill up and become pools of blessings.

You will go from strength to strength until you mount up with eagle wings-up,up,up to finally appear in My presence. For it is you dear suffering child, who receives strength from Me because in your suffering you are brought closer to Me.

Today your heart is sad. Come close to Me. There is a Glory Highway shining between you and Me- a band of light. Jacob saw it as a ladder, wherein angels ascended and descended, and standing on the other end of your Glory Highway; I am looking down on you to communicate with you as I did with Jacob. For I love you like I love Jacob. I have made a covenant with you as I have with Jacob, to do you good all the days of your life and to cause you to go from strength to strength.

E. God's Name Is Powerful! He is our banner! He is our peace! He is our all and all! Most people know Him and refer to Him as "God" which sounds so generic and distant. Yet if you study the names of God you will begin to see how personal He is. Jehovah is God of gods, and Lord of lords. "There is nothing too hard for thee." The name under which God made great and mighty promises, to Abraham, Isaac and to Jacob.(Genesis 17:1, 35:11) *"He is the God who keeps covenant and loving kindness with His servants who walk before Him with all their heart" (1 Kings 8:23).*

I believe He will keep his promise to Joe and me because we walk before him with our whole heart.

Examples Of God Keeping His Covenant

*Noah (Genesis 6:18), Examples of God keeping His covenant are found in Noah. He chose to obey God, even when people were laughing at him and scorning everything he did. Because Noah didn't listen to those around him and kept his eyes fixed on God and kept his heart toward God, He blessed his entire family.

*Abraham was blessed because he also **kept his heart and eyes fixed on God and the promise He gave him** (Genesis 17:1). If you read Hebrews chapter 11 you will read about so many other heroic men and women, who also kept their hearts and minds fixed on God and chose to obey Him.

God keeps His covenant with His people today. That's you and me! His covenant is promised to us and was sealed by the precious blood of Jesus. He will not change, He is eternal. Learn to keep your mind and heart fixed on His promises because they never change.

If you notice, **the Heroes of our Faith were Blessed Because They Kept Their Eyes Fixed on God, Walked in Obedience, and Chose to Obey Him and then Expected the Promise.** This is what we choose to do, **we will keep our hearts and minds fixed on God! And we will expect the promise!**

If you have noticed, God keeps His covenant with those servants who love Him and walk in His ways. He is unchanging and His Word remains forever. His Name is powerful. It is at the Name of Jesus every knee will bow and say He is Lord.

My husband and I choose to love the Lord and fear the Lord; we do not want to be like the Israelites who forgot what the Lord had done for them. We will remember all our miracles and will never turn away from God, or say that miracles are not for today. We fear the Lord and are committed to His ways.

Remember, the fear of the Lord is the beginning of wisdom. We will continue to bless the Lord every minute of our lives. Always remember to "bless the Lord at all times, and let His praise be on your lips" (Psalm 34:1).

Question: Will you forget the miracles God has done for you?

_____

_____

_____

Question: Will you praise the Lord even when you are discouraged?

_____

_____

_____

Ponder: God sees your misery, He hears you when you cry and He is concerned about your suffering. Exodus 3:7

Scripture to memorize: *"Let us fix our eyes on Jesus, the author and perfecter of our faith, who for the joy set before him endured the cross, scorning its shame, and sat down at the right hand of the throne of God" (Hebrew 12:2).*

Things to do: Study the Names of God:

Jehovah Nissi, Jehovah Rapha, Jehovah Jireh, Jehovah Shalom, Jehovah Tsidkenu..........

_____

_____

_____

CHAPTER 28

The Fear of the Lord is Wisdom

Progression

Understand that the hepatitis C virus is attacking Joe's liver again. Just because he has a new liver, doesn't rid him of the virus. In some cases, the recipient will be cleared of any signs of the virus and stay in stage 1 where the liver has only inflammation while other recipients will progress to cirrhosis again. My husband is back in stage 2-3 which only took him fifteen months after transplant!

This filthy spirit of infirmity must be stopped! I call it the "beast." It must be cast out in Jesus" Name! We will continue to fight this virus with the Spirit of God. When the family of God heard the news they lifted us up in prayer and began to fast again. Fasting and prayer are two of the biggest tools we have to fight against the enemy. Thank the Lord, for our prayer warriors who always uphold us.

Lesson #12 What Is The Fear Of The Lord? *"The fear of the Lord is an expression of your trust in Him."* Our minds *are made up that we love the Lord, and we will honor* Him no matter what the outcome. We have the victory. We win!

The Bible explains it this way: *"Come, my children, listen to me; I will teach you the fear of the Lord. Whoever of you loves life and desires to see many good days, keep your tongue from evil and your lips from speaking lies. Turn from evil and do good; seek peace and pursue it"* (Psalms 34:11, 12). *That verse is the fear of the Lord*

In our prayer time, we asked the Lord to teach us His wisdom to show us what to do because we know the wisdom of the Lord is eternal. *"Blessed is the man who finds wisdom, the man who gains understanding. For she is more profitable than silver and yields better returns than gold. She is more precious than rubies nothing you desire can compare with her. Long life is in her right hand, in her left hand are riches and honor"* (Proverbs 3:13).

Nutrition

As we prayed and ask the Lord for wisdom, He laid it on our heart to go back on the special diet which is mostly vegetables and fruit. Eating a healthy diet with good nutrition can help build new cells to regenerate the liver. Don't forget, the liver can regenerate.

If you must have meat only have it a few times a week, small amount and hormone free. Remember, when eating, you must lighten the work of the liver with liver friendly foods. Make sure you do not overwork the liver, as it has so many functions; and it's very important for it to rest. One of the best ways to do this is to go organic. Most foods are sprayed with toxic pesticides and you want to put less strain on the liver. I know this can be expensive so if you can't go organic on everything, use the vegetable and fruit cleaner. Make sure you soak your fruits and vegetables really well.

Please be advised not to take a heavy vitamin regimen unless you ask your doctor. However, my husband did a lot of research and found food based vitamins without iron worked well. Too much iron can be toxic to the liver.

He also did some research and found Alpha-lipoic acid fights off free radicals and helps to build cells. Please see your personal physician so they may direct you to the supplement program which is right for you; this is a very complicated disease and you should be under medical care.

My Journal: The medical doctors want Joe to begin treatment sometime soon, they have come out with some new treatments and we are waiting for them to say when to begin. They want his skin to clear up before he starts because it can make it worse. They say they will start him with a smaller dose of medicine and he has a better chance because he has a new liver. Although there is a chance of liver rejection and he would need another transplant! This time around is even more complicated than the first time because he's taking autoimmune suppressant medication. He may experience liver rejection or failure. This particular medication they want to treat him with still has Interferon in it which we really don't want to have. The nurse practitioner tried to put our mind at ease by telling us "not to worry if he has liver rejection because he will be virus free and can have a second transplant."

Honestly, I cannot even go there, I wish it were that simple! I've already been on that road, I know there are no livers available and he would need another live donor. Medically I can only donate once. We don't want to take the chance of rejection, but at the same time, the liver can be damaged by the virus. We will continue to trust the Lord for His direction. We choose to continue to trust the Lord and live by His direction and intervention. Our God can do the impossible! Our God can do the Impossible! When man can't, God can! My husband loves to say, "When man stops, God begins."

Again, Joe and I sat our daughters down to explain that daddy's new liver was being infected again by the virus. We knew they were older at this point, and would hear others talking with us. God gave us the ability to tell them in peace and strength. We talked about any concerns they had, prayed together and continued life as normal as possible.

Life Application: I have been told in the past that we are not living in reality. Let me share with you, we know all about living in reality. After all, I did donate my liver to my husband; however, Joe and I are not ruled by negative reports. We will always believe the report of the Lord.

Joe and I have spent many days crying out to the Lord for His intervention. I used that phrase many times during this book, I'd like to share an article that was placed in the SGT (Smithtown Gospel Tabernaclc) Happenings Magazine, it caught my attention when I saw the title, "Crying out to the Lord." It will explain the realities we live by.

Article: "Holy Scripture declares, "Evening and morning and at noon, I will pray and cry aloud and He shall hear my voice" Psalm 55:17. Crying out to the Lord brings prayer to a new level of intensity that translates into a deeper expression from your heart. It doesn't simply mean you become more emotional or louder it means you press into God with a greater passion and authenticity with a tenacious and focused spirit. Moreover, from a Biblical perspective,

"Crying Out To The Lord"
Incorporates Four Realities.

First, it expresses itself through **desperation**. Desperation is an intense acknowledgment that you need God's direct intervention stepping away from self-reliance and declaring absolute dependence upon God. This is not a call to personal passivity but passionate obedience to connect with God as your source. Second, crying out to the Lord incorporates **perspiration**-to intentionally and purposefully "work out" your commitment to look to the Lord and do life His way. Third, crying out to the Lord engenders **inspiration** by God's promises and is motivated to live life in anticipation of their fulfillment. And that leads to the fourth reality that emerges as an expression of crying out to the Lord; namely, **expectation**. Expectation is your hope, faith, and confidence being rooted solely in God with a sense of waiting for His amazing and magnificent faithfulness to manifest. God's faithfulness and power will literally explode into your life and situation as you "cry out to Him!" Written by: - Pastor Gary Zarlengo. [6]

As you read this article I pray you will have a clearer understanding as to the reality Joe and I live by. We will continue to "stand by faith and not by sight." We will continue to acknowledge we are desperate for God's direct intervention and that we have total dependence on Him.

If anyone knows about living in reality, it is Joe and I; our minds are made up we will not be ruled by fear! We believe in His mighty power to save and to heal which He already paid for. We also know God does use medicine and the medical field and the brilliance of the doctors who He gave His wisdom to.

Joe was supposed to start treatment soon, but Praise the Lord his numbers are going down. His virus load went from eight million to eight hundred thousand. The count is still high but substantially lower. ALT and AST

---

[6] Pastor Gary Zarlengo: Smithtown, Gospel Tabernacle "Happenings Magazine"

went from the two hundreds to the low seventies,doctors want to wait for Joe to begin treatment.

We also couldn't begin the medicine because my husband broke out with the shingles after retiring from his job.

There have been so many miracles in our life; I have to share them with you to encourage you to trust the Lord with everything. Thank the Lord for the job he had which has been a blessing to us in so many ways. God even cared about that! He cares about everything life may bring.

He was the Spanish speaking drug counselor for sixteen years for Suffolk County. He went back to work after the transplant for eight months, but when he was diagnosed again, he was forced to retire and then he broke out with the shingles. The shingles is a very, very painful nerve and skin disorder. Joe didn't think he was stressing over retirement; however, his body showed otherwise. I don't think it was only over retirement but also the thoughts of losing his liver and going through the same procedure again!

I know Joe has asked the Lord to either heal him or take him home, but he does not want to go through end stage liver failure again. Nor does he want his family to experience the same pain. Don't think this is a selfish prayer. I'm okay with that because I don't want to see him or our family go through that painful state again either. We have in our heart, given everything to the Lord. Though painful, yet reality.

The shingles lasted for months and so did his skin condition. We found that using lemon balm directly on the skin caused the shingles not to blister and dried up quicker. Due to the shingles, the doctors had him on prednisone, and after he was on that for months and came off his skin broke out with a very bad condition of psoriasis, almost like boils. He felt like Job scratching the boils from his skin. The doctors did not want him to begin treatment until his skin healed because the medication could make it worse and also because his numbers were decreasing.

Truthfully, we don't want to take the medication anyway. We find it easier to trust God with his life rather than being on this medication.

Every day is a day to have faith and trust in the Lord. The doctors are amazed that his numbers are going down even though he is not on the medicine and are asking what we attribute this to. We attribute this to the Lord and His mighty power; his mighty power to save and to heal. The Lord placed this song on my heart, sing to him a new song "God is faithful! He is faithful, He will never, never leave you alone, God is faithful, He's so faithful, and He will guide you all the time. Even when we can't see it, even when we don't understand, God is faithful, he's so faithful, put your trust in Him. He knows better than we know all though sometimes it makes no sense. That's where trusting in Him is so important, put your life in His hands and He will lead and guide you all the time, He is faithful to His Word and promises. He is faithful to His words and promises all the time."

CHAPTER 29

The Fruit of Your Heart

There continues to be no treatment for Joe; it is 2011, we are beginning to see signs of irritability, mood swings, and nervousness. This is all caused by hepatitis C and the many medications he is taking. I'm also watching for water gain, yellowish eyes, and dark urine. It is once again, a stressful time in our life. I'm going to explain to you how we continued to hold on and grow in the midst of this new test. During this time of trusting God, I had to draw closer to the Lord for He is my answer, my comforter, and my peace.

Lesson # 13 We Cannot Demand That God Change Things or Get Mad At Him If It Stays The Same: We must humble ourselves and ask the Lord to change us into His image so that we can grow in the process. The way you can do this is by laying all your cares and concerns at the foot of the cross. He wants you to cast all your cares upon Him.

A. We Need to Be In His Perfect Will For Our Lives: As long as we are willing to complete His call in our lives and to always give Him the glory, He will see you through. God is looking for us to be obedient in every part of our life. If you noticed throughout my book the level of obedience has gone higher and higher. The level of faith has grown in different levels. God is bringing us to maturity and it comes by obedience. It's easy to say no, I will do it my way, but the negative price you have to pay is far greater.

We all have the potential to overcome, some may give up and become bitter and some may grow by their circumstances and become a better person. I will continue to choose life and grow and become better. You have the power to choose.

Life Application: Have a yielded, willing heart toward the Holy Spirit and allow Him to mold and shape you. Stay obedient and willing to walk through the challenge. No matter how many times you may ask the Lord to remove certain situations from your life, He may allow it to remain because you are being tried and tested. Look at the apostle Paul. He asked the Lord three times to remove the thorn in his side and the answer *was "My grace is sufficient for you, for my power is made perfect in weakness" (2 Corinthians 12:9).*

Instead of wanting the situation to change, ask the Holy Spirit to change you. Ask Him to help you walk through the challenge with victory. Then your response will be positive and by doing this, your character is being proven and built to become stronger.

If we are going to go through these difficult times let's look at the ways it will help us to become a better person or have a stronger relationship with God. Sometimes it's easy and other times, it's hard and painful. However, He always makes us triumph through Him. I love the way the Living Bible reads, *"Dear brothers, is your life full of difficulties and temptations? Then be happy, for when the way is rough, your patience has a chance to grow. So let it grow and don't try to squirm out of your problems. For when your patience is finally in full bloom, then you will be ready for anything, strong in character, full and complete" (James 1:2-4, TLB).*[7]

It kind of makes me laugh, "Is your life full of difficulties and temptations (problems) then be happy!" The best choice is to be happy through it all so that why?

We Can Be Ready For Anything, Strong In Character

B. **Your Character Determines Your Responses;** everyone has responses; good or bad, positive or negative. If we read Galatians chapter 5 you will understand what positive and negative responses are. Verse 16 says, *"So I say, live by the Spirit and you will nor gratify the desires of the sinful nature."* The word *"nature"* refers to our *"character."* *"For the sinful nature desires what is contrary to the Spirit and the Spirit what is contrary to the sinful nature. They are in*

---

[7] Living Bible copyright 1971 by Tyndale House Foundation

conflict with each other, they do not do as you want"
(Galatians 5:17, NIV).

Life Application: When we live by the Spirit we will not gratify our sinful nature. How do you live by the Spirit? By making a choice to walk according to His Word. You will be full of Him and not yourself, you will be able to live a life of faith rather than a life of the flesh. We must be rooted and established in love so that we can be strengthened with His power through the Holy Spirit in our inner being.

When we do this then we can understand and grasp how wide, long, and deep the love of Christ is. Then, we will know He is able to do *"immeasurably more than all we ask or imagine; according to His power that is at work within us"* (Ephesians 3:20), did you see it? According to "His" power that is at work within us. It's not by your might, your power, but by His power in us. This is why He wants us to be in Him. The more we are in Him, rooted and grounded and He is in us, the less we have to fear and the more we can triumph. *"These things have I spoken to you, that My joy may remain in you, and that your joy may be full"* (John 15:11, NIV). He wants your joy to be full.

Our roots need to be deep in God so that our attitude will be one of honor. When your character is true then the attitude of your heart is purified. How is it purified? By rain!

Life Application: The rain comes when there is a storm or a cloudy day. (Trials of life) When the sun is not shining, when it's dark, cloudy, dreary, the rain comes but its job is one of extreme importance. Without the rain things won't grow, everything will dry up and die. I love how everything looks after it rains; all my flowers and all the plants look so green and strong. They look nourished.

This is the same thing in our life, the rain will come to cause us to grow so that we may become mature and complete. Let's look at this rain as the "son" shower.

Even though it may be raining in your life, you can see the light of the Lord guiding you. As we come filled with the water of Life, we will never thirst again. He quenches our thirst as we become full of the water which is the Spirit of God. Jesus promised when He rose again and descended to Heaven, He would not leave us alone, He would send the Comforter, the Holy Spirit to come and live in you. He will direct your life and lead you into all truth. If the Holy Spirit lives in you walk as a child of the King, He will give you the strength to do so.

Become like the tree who grows during the rain; what does Jesus tell us? *"Come to me, those who are thirsty and you will never thirst again."* When the Holy Spirit comes, you will be refreshed as the rain refreshes the earth. If you have lost hope, you will be refreshed to believe again. Then the fruit will grow and blossom so that it will touch other lives and yours for the best. How do you touch other lives? By love, the greatest fruit there is love.

"If We Haven't Done It In Love, We Haven't Done It At All" (1 Corinthians 13).

That is a huge checkpoint in my life. It's hard to show love when there is a hurt or a broken heart. When your heart is torn and it feels broken, only Jesus can heal your deepest pain. You can't take a pill to heal a broken heart, not even a medical doctor can cure a broken heart, Only God!

Maybe you have experienced this deep painful hurt and you feel like you can't go on. Give your pain to Jesus. Only He can restore and make you whole. I can't explain how He does this, all I can say is He pours His healing balm on your sores and they begin to heal either step by step or instantly.

There is a time to heal! Ecclesiastes 3:1-4 says, *"There is a time for everything and a season for every activity under heaven. A time to be born and a time to die. A time to plant and a time to uproot. A time to kill and a time to heal. A time to tear down and a time to build. A time to weep and a time to laugh."*

Laughter may seem like it will never come again, but it will. God will make everything beautiful in His time.

Question: How do you respond to the Lord when things don't go your way?

Question: Will you walk away from God and His Word? Even when it hurts and you don't understand? Or will you draw closer to Him?

_____

_____

_____

CHAPTER 30

The Fruit of the Spirit

The fruit of our heart is connected to the fruit of the Spirit! Our heart is so important because it determines our actions, and our actions prove what's in our heart. This is what our Christian character must be established in. Let me share it with you, remember, apart from Him you can't do it.

A. Love: If we look at the first commandment it says, *"Love the Lord your God with all your heart, and with all your soul and with all your mind and the second is like it. Love your neighbor as yourself" (Matthew 22:34-39)*. If everyone truly walked in these commandants imagine the world!

B. Joy: Is truly not based on material happiness. It's an inner peace only found in Christ. Joy comes when you are walking and living in Gods will for your life. The joy of the Lord is our strength and that is what keeps us and gives us the inner strength to hold on while you wait for your miracle.

C. Peace: Is true life; having peace with God, yourself and mankind. Not having any ill feelings in your heart, resting in God knowing he will take care of you. Also, I shared with you about the true peace that surpasses all understanding.

D. **Patience:** My whole story is about having patience. Patience is something we all need to practice. Waiting for your prayers to be answered; without being impatient.

E. **Kindness:** Helping others with any task, being considerate of others feelings before your own.

F. **Gentleness**: When I think about gentleness, I think about my mom. Speaking in a soft tone of voice, not wanting to bring anyone harm, always forgiving and walking in humility and meekness. Remember, "Meekness is not weakness; it is the power of God unto salvation".

G. **Faithfulness**: God is faithful; He keeps His promise!" He will never leave you or forsake you".

H. **Self-Control**: Keeping your tongue, thoughts, and actions under the authority of Christ.

I. **Goodness**: Walking in love, respect, and dignity. God is good all the time. We need to follow His example.

What I love about the Fruit of the Spirit is it gives us a guideline to follow. Walking in the Spirit and trying to live by His example is truly demonstrating Self-Control. When we go wrong, the Spirit convicts us and if we love God and repent we will be quick to change our actions and behavior. Remember, the fruit of the Spirit will help us to walk in the midst of a chaotic life. Blessings will follow.

"Blessed is the man who does not walk in the counsel of the wicked or stand in the way of sinners or sit in the seat of mockers But his delight is in the law of the Lord, and on his law he meditates day and night. He is like a tree planted by streams of water which yields its fruit in season and whose leaf does not wither. Whatever he does prospers" (Psalms 1:1-3).

The fruit the Lord is talking about is the fruit of our heart. Joe and I both had to check our hearts, especially at a time like this. Were we going to become angry and resentful? After all, we just went through a major transplant. Or were we going to trust God and continue our journey with joy and victory? We feared the Lord; and decided to continue to walk in the fruit of the Spirit despite the evidence of the negative report and possibly heading toward end stage liver failure again.

Life Application: In the previous verse I quoted, did you notice it says, "If we trust the Lord and our confidence is in Him, we will be like a tree planted by water"?

This is an analogy of who we are. Jesus wants us to bear fruit from our tree, which is our life; sometimes, the leaves on our tree become strong and vibrant and produce its fruit in the proper season."

It's interesting to me they use the word "season" I know we all have different seasons during our lifetime, sometimes it seems like there is different fruit growing on our tree during different seasons in our life. Sometimes our fruit is vibrant in color (*self-control, patience, gentleness, kindness*) and other times it looks a little rotten and falls to the ground (*bitterness, anger, resentment, jealousy, fits of rage*). When our fruit if rotten, the gardener, who is our Father, sees certain fruit coming out of our tree (life) and prunes us so that we fully grow and mature. Without it we stagnate and die and never grow and flourish.

Jesus is calling us to live in Him, if you want Him to direct your path your roots must be submerged in Him. You must be so close to Him that He is in you and you are in Him. When you do this you will not fear when the year of drought comes. This is how we will be able to go through hardships with joy and have Godly character, by relying on God and imitating the character of Jesus.

Our character is not just what we try to display for others to see, it is who we are even when no one is watching. Good character is doing the right things because it is the thing to do. Good fruit or corrupt fruit will grow from your tree which is symbolizing you! What are you doing behind closed doors when no one is watching?

Doesn't God say in *John 15:1 "I am the true vine, and my Father is the gardener? He cuts off every branch in me that bears no fruit while every branch that does bear fruit He prunes so that it will be even more fruitful?"* He doesn't prune us because He wants to torture us. He prunes us because He loves us.

The Father prunes us because of His love for us." *No discipline seems pleasant at the time, but painful. Later on, however, it produces a harvest of righteousness and peace for those who have been trained by it."* (*Hebrews*

12:11) *Read those words again and take a moment and meditate on that scripture.* **"It produces a harvest of righteousness for those who have been trained by it."** Read all of Hebrew 12.

An example of the effects of pruning is taking care of rose bushes. Every few weeks I have to prune them and cut off the dead branches after I do this I find an abundance of buds on the bush. This helps them to flourish throughout the summer.

God does the same thing. He is the gardener. He prunes us for correction, notice the promise of God, "If we don't lose heart and we have a yielded heart to Him our leaf will never wither and whatever we do will prosper." He wants us to prosper but we must abide in Him. He is the El-Shaddai, Almighty God is all sufficient and all bountiful, the source of all blessings, fullness, and fruitfulness. "He is able to do exceedingly abundantly above all that we can think of or imagine." God wants to bless His children, although He also chastens those He loves. El-Shaddai is also used in connection with judging, chastening, purging. He purges us to bring us closer to Him. He wants our lives to flourish, but sometimes it takes the chastening of the Lord to bring us to the place of surrender so that we may flourish. He wants our fruit in our lives to emulate Him.

My husband and I are learning all the fruit, especially patience, believe me, I'd rather learn it in a different way, but again His ways are higher than ours. We know the truth and that is God is sovereign and He knows all things. We have come to the point in our life that we are grateful for every day He has given us. When He decides it is time to go home then so be it! We will bless the Lord. I'm not saying there won't be tears and grieving, but we know it will be in His will and the proper time, there will be no fear, but confidence in the Lord. When we humble ourselves before the Lord, He will bless us.

Obedience comes when you truly desire to do the will of your Father. I can think of many instances in my life that God called me to be obedient to His will and because I love Him and wanted to obey Him, I humbled myself and completed what He asked. Not because I was able to in my own ability, but because I asked the Lord to give me the strength to be able to complete His will. Sometimes I asked the Lord to make His will become mine.

If your heart is not pliable you will want to run and do things your own way.

**He's God, Who Can Identify With
Everything You Are Going Through
And He Will Direct You.**

Question: Are you able to rejoice during your problems and trials? Knowing your patience is being developed?

_____

_____

Question: What fruit are you growing?

_____

_____

Debra Lynn Viteri

Heavenly Father,
I ask you to give my dear reader the strength to endure their trials so they may have the grace and ability to continue to cry out to You. That they may be able to walk in firmness and steadfastness not being moved by circumstances.

CHAPTER 31

Choose to Trust Him

One day I was driving to work and all of a sudden I felt anxiety come upon me. I began to feel overwhelmed because Joe was seeing the doctor in the city and we were waiting for some reports on his blood work. I began to feel nervous and a sense of distraction and fear tried to grip me. Immediately His Word went through my mind, and out my mouth, I quoted, "Thank You, Lord, I give You my anxiety, *"I cast all my anxiety on you, for you care for me" (1 Peter 5:7)*. The minute I spoke the Word I felt a release. As I continued to speak the Word over again and proclaimed, "Jesus is the author and finisher of my faith," I received peace and joy.

When I feel discouraged I: speak to my soul and command it to rise up and praise the Lord anyway. This is another devotional from Gwen Shaw that speaks about having your soul rise up. It blessed me; I pray it will bless you.

Devotional: *"Why Art Thou Cast Down O My Soul?"*

"Why art thou cast down, O my soul? And why art thou disquieted within me? Hope in God: for I shall yet praise him who is the health of my countenance, and my God." (Psalm 43:5) It is good to ask yourself this same question. Why is your soul cast down? Have you taken your eyes off Me, your Lord? Do you think that I have stopped leading you with my light and truth? Why are you disquieted within your soul? Have you lost your faith and hope in Me? Have you lost that unique, simple, childlike trust you used to have? Why are you disquieted within your soul? Do you think I don't love you as much as I did? Do you think that I am not the same mighty, powerful God that I was to you in the days gone by? Why are you cast down, dear soul? It is only because you have allowed your heart to become troubled and entangled too much with the things of this world. Your mind has dwelt on the negative. The doubts of others and their wrongdoings have oppressed you. Forget about them. Think about My greatness. Count your blessings I have given you in the past. I have never failed you and I never shall. I shall always be with you. I shall always protect you, lead you and guide you. And you shall go to My altar and shall make sweet music unto Me. And you shall praise Me, because I, alone, am your exceeding joy, and if it is true that I am your exceeding joy, then why is your soul disquieted within you? Let Me fulfill every need of your life. And, then you shall be full of joy and you shall praise Me, and I will be the health and the glory of your countenance, and your God.

While walking through my darkest valley, I chose to trust Him and praise Him. I believe God cares for the troubles of each of His children, He wants us to give all our concerns to Him so that He will take care of us. His desire is for you to have a heart of trust. This can happen by casting all your anxiety on Him. God wants to take your heart and make it a heart of flesh which feels and is sensitive toward God and His ways. It's pliable to change and is always looking to please God to be obedient. He's the only one who can search the heart. He will help you to be humble. Humility is what the Lord is looking for; there will be no growth unless there is humility.

"Only the pure in heart shall see God" (Matthew 5:8). That is why I always mentioned we have to have a pure heart before God.

Your faith must be proven genuine and the result is praise, glory and honor to Jesus Christ. The opposite of faith is fear, fear will become worry, and worry will become lack of peace. Satan wants to steal your peace. There have been many days my husband was being robbed of his peace.

"My illness has overwhelmed me; it's robbing my peace and stealing my joy. My mind is preoccupied with dying and leaving my family. There is no peace in my life. I cannot go through this again, please Lord, heal me or take me home. There is only turmoil inside of me. I can't sleep at night; my mind is being tormented day and night. Please, Lord, help me."

Don't allow yourself to be tormented. It's very real, we lived through it, however, Satan has no power over you unless you let him. There were nights Joe had to wake me to pray over him and the minute we prayed and cast out the spirit of fear, he would fall asleep in peace.

Many of you have lost your peace, your hope while going through your storms of life. I will share with you about restoring your peace.

There Are Four Principles You Must Put Into Practice

1. God's Priorities: Your priorities must line up with God's. Ask yourself if what is valuable to you is also valuable to God? Clarify what is important; make sure they are God's priorities. How are you using your time? What words are you speaking? What thoughts are you thinking? You can choose who and what you focus on. You can't control the storm, but you can control your thinking. When you do this, here is the promise God gives you. *"You will keep in perfect peace him whose mind is steadfast because he trusts in you"* (Isaiah 26:3).

There are so many truths to practice and take to heart. One major area we have to change is our thinking. I've said it before and I will say it again. When we are cast down it is because we have allowed our minds to get entangled with the things of this world. We have decided what dictates our emotions. I have gotten to this place several times, feeling burdened with life's cares. When I decide to change my thinking toward the Lord, my whole countenance changes and I then I was able to walk in victory and peace. Let us count our blessings and name them one by one you will be amazed of the faith you will receive.

2. God's Protection: I know sometimes it feels like God is a million miles away while you're going through your situations, however, if you can keep your mind focused on the fact that, *"He will never leave you or forsake you"(Joshua 1:5)*. He's already with you. He has a hedge of protection around you.

There is an analogy I heard many years ago when I felt like God was nowhere to be found. Picture God in the driver's seat, you're in the passenger seat of a car. The person driving never moves, they are in control of the car. He never moved away, it was me who moved. As I reached out to Him, He was right there. The more you get closer to Him; He will remain close to you. He's already with you. When you get those negative thoughts that say, "Lord where are You?" Instead, say, "Thank You Lord for being by my side and for directing me." "Thank You for never leaving me." Thank You for directing my every step." Thank You that You are in control and that You will protect me." At night, you can rest assured that He has you covered. His promise is *"I will lie down and sleep in peace, for you alone, O Lord, make me dwell in safety"* (Psalm 4:8).

3. God's Purpose: The Lord wants you to know that even though you can't see it and there may be large clouds in the way of your sight, He has a plan and purpose for your life. There is no storm that can blow away your purpose. You can choose to feel sorry for yourself or you can choose to believe God. God's purposes stand firm forever and won't be blown away. Continue to believe that there is an ultimate purpose that you will fulfill. God's promise *"I will instruct you (says the Lord) and guide you along the best pathway for your life; I will advise you and watch your progress"* (Psalm 32:8).

4. God's Promises: All these scriptures you have read throughout this book are God's promises to us, God cannot lie. As you thank Him for your peace of mind and heart, He will give you peace that surpasses all understanding. This peace will come not from a martini or by a prescription drug, but by God Himself. You will be clear-minded and alert.

Continue to hold fast to the promises of God. He will not fail you; His Word is true. He is faithful to all He loves.

Peace with God is a wonderful benefit we receive. There are so many people today that are living and trying to fulfill their lives with earthly pleasures, yet they feel empty. This is because they have no peace with God, our Creator. Peace with God is a blessing. He wants to impart to you. When we accept His gift of eternal life, freedom will come and therefore you will be able to rejoice in God. We can rejoice in the love of God. We can see the character of God, His love, mercy and forgiving us as sinners, and because He chooses to forgive us, He can reconcile us back to Himself. *"Peace I leave with you: my peace I give you. I do not give to you as the world gives. Do not let your hearts be troubled and do not be afraid"* (John 14:27).

The peace you are reading about is "peace with God through our Lord Jesus Christ." This peace comes to man how? When he trusts in Jesus Christ, the Messiah, as Savior and knows that God no longer has any charge against him. This peace comes knowing that your sins are forgiven and that everything comes right between you and God. You are now right-standing, made righteous. Peace with God meaning that God has nothing against you. He is our peace; Jehovah Shalom. The Hebrew word for *peace* is *Shalom*. This word translates to *"harmony, wholeness, soundness, well-being and success* in all areas of your life."

This is exactly what the God of peace wants for you. He wants you to have success in every area of your life. He will give you peace of mind. Without peace, you lose your strength and give into the storm. Worry, anxiety, and fear will zap you of your strength. Without peace, you lose your way. You will make your decisions out of fear instead of faith. You lose your direction when you lose your direction you lose all hope.

I am here to tell you God has made a way where there seems to be no way. You can restore your peace. "Thou oh Lord art a shield about me and the glory of the lifter of my head." He has a shield around you to protect you. Remember, lift up your shield of faith, and don't be afraid, He will give you the grace to walk in victory no matter what. God's promise is *"Let him have all your worries and cares, for he is always thinking about you and watching everything that concerns you" (1 Peter 5:7, TLB).*

CHAPTER 32

Character Building

From the beginning of this book in 2003, here I am continuing to write about our story through our Journey with hepatitis C. It continues to be 2011, there continues to be no medication for Joe, and there is nothing the doctors can do to stop the liver from progressing to fibrosis which will lead to cirrhosis again. It's been three years since the transplant and one and a half years since his last biopsy. I can get overwhelmed during this time thinking about his liver progressing quickly, but I choose to continue to trust and gain wisdom and strength from the Word. This time with a larger vision and more understanding; I can see clearer!

This testing of my faith has developed perseverance in me, and in my husband. Trials build character, sharpen your character and fine tune your character. Your character cannot be tested until you go through trials

Character Building

Life Application: Why is God so interested in building our character? Our character is so important because your character will determine your future and outcome either for the positive or negative depending on the response you reveal. Your character can either break or make you. Good character is a Godly response regardless of difficulties; it helps us to be stable and to be built into a greater vessel full of strength.

Your attitude controls your character and your character controls what people see, either positive or negative. Joy, peace, patience or anger, bitterness, resentment.

After Joe was diagnosed again, we could have responded negatively and angrily. We could have been resentful and bitter. Instead, we held onto God's grace and continued to have confidence in Him in spite of our difficulties. We were being built and made stronger through our adversity. Our character was growing into a maturity level that rose beyond circumstances. It wasn't easy, but we were determined to live by Jerimiah 17:7-8.

"Blessed is the man who trusts in the Lord, whose confidence is in him. He will be like a tree planted by the water that sends out its roots by the stream. It does not fear when heat comes; its leaves are always green. It has no worries in a year of drought and never fails to bear fruit" (Jerimiah 17:7-8).

Every time you trust the Lord, you are extending your roots in faith. It may be painful, and you may not see immediate results, but continue to trust the Lord. If you do this, you will not fear when the heat comes (trials of life) because your roots are extending to the water which is truly symbolizing the Holy Spirit. You will be rooted and grounded in Christ. But, look what happens when you don't trust the Lord.

"Cursed is the one who trusts in man, who depends on flesh for his strength and whose heart turns away from the Lord. He will be like a bush in the wastelands; he will not see prosperity when it comes. He will dwell in the parched places of the desert, in a salt land where no one lives" (Jeremiah 17: 5-6).

In the beginning of my book, you read how I was being tossed by the wind of doubt and fear; I knew I needed my roots to become deeper. Going through all these challenges has definitely made me deeper in my faith and greatly rooted. Purpose in your heart you never want to turn away from the Lord, but you will trust Him.

Lesson # 14 Valley Experience: It is the valley experiences that God can build character into your life. When we go into the valley, they are not to break us, (to keep us broken), but to make us. I have to tell you that after going through this for several years, both Joe and I would not change the valley experience because we have learned so much. It's in those times we see God's hand at work and how much He loves us.

In the beginning of this book I quoted "Consider it pure joy, my brothers, whenever you face trials of many kinds, because you know that the testing of your faith produces perseverance. Perseverance must finish its work so that you may be mature and complete, not lacking anything" (James 1:2).

I had a hard enough time reading the word "joy"; but now as I look back and really read the Scripture, it not only says consider it joy, but pure joy.

A. **Pure:** when you think of the word pure what comes to your mind? Crystal clear, wholeness, undefiled, free from pollution comes to my mind. When you mix joy with doubt and fear you are polluting it and it is not pure. Pure joy can only be found in Him, it's not based on materialistic things, and it doesn't come from feelings, emotions, or earthly possessions. Pure joy is a joy that says to be content in all situations; it helps us to rise above all your emotional feelings, all your inadequacies. It's a joy that comes with no strings attached, a joy that is holy and pure found only in Christ, whose word says to us *"The joy of the Lord is our strength"* (Nehemiah 8:9). In Him, there is fullness of joy completeness. If you grasp the fullness of His joy you will be complete in every aspect of your life.

B. **Joy:** In myself and my own emotions pure joy almost seemed impossible, but as I continued to keep my eyes and heart fixed on the Lord, He gave me a song and the endurance to overcome. When I think of the joy of the Lord and that He has great and mighty plans for me and my husband; it makes me cheerful and helps me to rejoice. "Rejoice, for the steps of the righteous man are ordered of God." *"Rejoice greatly, with exceeding joy, because the testing of your faith "produces" perseverance" (James 1:3).*

Here's another devotional you may like to read about how the Lord guides our steps.

Devotional: *"I Am Guiding You Step By Step" (Psalm 37:23, 24)*

The good man is a very special person in My eyes and in My heart. He is one who is valiant, dedicated and strong through My Spirit working in him. This man is an honor to My name, for he walks with a listening ear, always ready to obey My Spirit Who dwells in him. The steps, actions and even the very thoughts of such a man are ordered, established, guided by Me. I lead him every step of the way and every hour of the day.

He is my friend, and as friends we not only walk together, we also talk together and have sweet communion along the way. This kind of relationship I desire to have with you, but you must take time to be with Me. I love you and I know you love Me, but you don't take the time to show Me your love nor tell Me you love Me, so sometimes, because you lag behind and follow at a distance, you fall. But because there is good in you and because My Spirit still dwells in you, you will rise again a little more humble, a little more grateful and a lot more loving and understanding, for you will have a heart filled with compassion And this time, you will reach out to hold My hand and I will uphold you by the words of My love, for you are a good man and I love you and will lead you every step of your life's way.

Allow this devotional to give you a desire to spend more time with the Lord because He truly does love you and when you do, you will be able to rejoice through life's trials. I'm going to take a few pages and go over some words I have been challenged by in the last few years, especially since Joe's last biopsy didn't come out as we expected.

I spoke to you about the testing of your faith throughout this book and we all know about perseverance, but what about those little words in between that sometimes get lost. The testing of your faith PRODUCES or DEVELOPS perseverance. God wants us to persevere which will help us to produce /develop those muscles of faith.

When I read my story, I can truly see my muscles of faith at work. I can see how much I have learned and how much I have grown.

C. **Development:** Development is a growth process that the Lord takes you through. This will bring you to the place where you can stand strong filled with courage, zeal, faith, and trust. He desires for you to be stronger, bigger and more advanced; so that you can walk in the fruit of the Spirit in victory.

If you notice, the words *"produce/develop* "is linked to perseverance.

"Persevere Under Trial and It Will Take You Where Nothing Else Will"

If you give up, you never know what the outcome would have been. When something becomes bigger and more advanced what does it do? What happens? Your perseverance, endurance, long-suffering, patience, steadfastness becomes active and you become more than capable, you are more than a conqueror to be able to persevere through your test and come out in victory with singing, dancing, and rejoicing.

D. Perseverance: God gives you the ability to "press on" so that your character develops or produces you into a person who can stand strong and vibrant no matter what the test, no matter what the trial. *"Not only so, but we also rejoice in our sufferings, because we know that suffering produces perseverance, perseverance character, character hope, And hope does not disappoint us, because God has poured out his love into our hearts by the Holy Spirit, whom he has given us" (Romans 5:3).*

If you allow it, God's grace will help you in the middle of your trial and it will also lead us to seek God more earnestly. I found this to be true in my own life. When we seek God more earnestly it produces perseverance in us which produces proven character and a hope to continue to believe. Proven character results in hope that does not disappoint us, a hope that does not give up. God's grace helps us to look beyond our present problems to a fervent hope in God. It gives you a determination which helps you to look beyond your trial and brings you to maturity and completeness. Then it goes on to say,

E. **Patience:** Let patience have its complete work in you through the workings of the Fruit of the Spirit. Maturity is what it's about; growing in the Lord so that when your patience is in full bloom you will be ready for anything. You would have reached your goal, fully grown, mature, complete, perfect, and lacking nothing. I see it as wholeness.

Patience only grows under trials. That is why most people never pray for patience. Patience can only be produced or developed through trials. In the book of James, He talks about having patience, "for when the way is rough your patience has a chance to grow."

F. **Endurance**: Is another part of my character trait God has been teaching me. Endurance is strength. "Jesus endured the cross (His trial) for the joy that was set before Him". My husband had to endure His cross of constant lies in his mind. Also, from the doctor when he was told there were no livers available, for him to find one or there was no hope of his survival. He had to endure the test that was set before him. You must have endurance in this life; to be strong, and to run the race and not give up!

How does this take place? By crying out to the Lord for His strength to be humble, obedient, yielded, and submitted to His ways; and by being willing to say, yes Lord, let Your will be done not mine. It's all about having Gods will in your life not your own; then you will be able to endure.

His will is always to heal, although I know too well that healing comes in many ways. It's not easy to submit, to yield and to be obedient; it's not easy to be patient. Many of us don't like those words; however, by doing this is where you will find peace and joy to overcome. You won't be beating around a bush but you will trust the Lord that His ways are perfect. Laying your own emotions on the side and learning to be selfless instead of selfish.

Are you emotionally stable? It's okay to struggle with doubt and unbelief but ask God to build unmovable faith into your spirit. Determine you will grow regardless of your situation and through your trial, you will not be easily moved. Your trials may be complex and of a greater magnitude than mine. Allow the Holy Spirit, the one who is our great source of comfort to bring you courage and healing in your heart right now. He will give you the ability to become stable again, filled with a new sense of direction and purpose for your life from what has transpired.

Priscilla Boos, my aunt, is a perfect example of this. She lost her husband only a few years ago. She could have stayed in the state of depression, but instead she got up, began to write her experience and is now an author of the book "Meet Me at the Bakery." God is now using her to bring God's comfort to those who are suffering from grief. Isn't that what it's about? Helping others? We are called to help others with the same comfort He has given us. God is calling us to lay down our lives for Him.

We Love You

My Journal: This morning May 5, seemed like any other morning. Joe, Jessica and I were relaxing by our pool and enjoying the sun when we received a phone call from one of Joe's brothers. His father has been rushed to the hospital for emergency surgery. Joe and I jumped in the car and sped to the hospital to see Pop lying in the hospital bed suffering from a fall on his head and a blood clot in his brain. Joe stayed at the hospital comforting his family and sitting by his father's side day and night just like he did for him years before. We both went to see him on Mother's day, I didn't mind being there, I wanted to be with my husband and my father-in-law. It was beautiful to see how Joe sat by his side and read him the Spanish and English Bible for hours. Even though Pop was unresponsive it brought peace in the room and who knows, he could have heard every word. I watched my husband shave his dad gently and took the time to love his father. We wanted him to get better and come home to be with his wife and family. However, God wanted him by His side.

When Joe gave a beautiful eulogy at his father's funeral I couldn't help but think about my father- in- law's heart's desire when he sat at Joe's bedside and said, "No son of mine is going before me." God heard his cry, and even though it has been difficult to say good-bye, I can't help but give thanks to the Lord for answering my father-in-law's prayer.

Question: Take a moment to ponder on a situation you are in. Do you see yourself as stable?

_____

_____

Not easily moved by circumstances?

Regardless or In Spite Of Situations In Your Life?

_____

_____

CHAPTER 33

Over Coming Battle Scars

Joseph was tried to the limit and was restored by God. I've seen my husband as Joseph for many years. Being tried and tested, not only with his health but as an employee. There were times that he was falsely accused and the Lord would always allow him to come out as a shining star. In fact, at one meeting his boss, not knowing, spoke prophetically to him about being a shining star (1 Peter 1:19).

"He sent a man before them, even Joseph, who was sold for a servant: Whose feet they hurt with fetters; he was laid in iron: Until the time that His word came: the word of the Lord tried him" (Psalm 105:17-19).

The purpose of God's character building is to develop Godly values so that you will flourish and live a life that will complete the calling of God in a successful manner; which will bring glory to Him. God had a plan for Joseph's character refinement, He used the wicked plans of his brothers; It was not by mistake that Joseph was sold as a slave.

Being sold as a slave by his own brothers seemed to be the cruelest punishment anyone could ever receive by his own flesh and blood. Can you imagine that was in the plan of God? How could it be? The worst judgment for any human being and that was in God's plan? If you really look at the story, Jacob loved Joseph more than any of his sons, he would have been spoiled; his character would have been self-centered. God saw his tenacious spirit and said, "I'm going to use this man for My good and My purposes for My Kingdom." Even centuries and years later, Joseph is known throughout the world and for many generations. Movies have been made from his story, children's books have been written to teach the little ones about the faithfulness of God in Joseph's life. Preachers have taught on his story to encourage their congregations. Did he know back then the impact of his sufferings would have on billions of people years later? Never did he ever know what his life would do for humanity.

God knew that even before Joseph was born and his mother died, He had a specific plan for his life to save not only his family from famine but the entire nation of Egypt and Israel.

By saving his family the promise of God was preserved.

Joseph was not only tried and tested by being sold but then being accused falsely by Potiphar's wife of rape. To prevent his character from being destroyed, God had a plan for his life, and He allowed him to be cast into prison. Imagine being thrown into prison for something you didn't do? What was he thinking? God where are You? I've been good all my life; I've served You the best way I know how. My own brothers sold me and now I'm cast into prison! Thanks God! He felt disowned, rejected, and lonely with no hope of release.

Does that sound familiar? God, where are You? I've served You the best way I know how, why is this happening to me? Can you imagine?, being thrown in prison was in God's plan? We can never see the plan while we are going through the trial; however, there's always a reason for what we are going through. Something good will always come out of it.

Years later, God filled Joseph's mind with prophetic dreams and visions. Joseph was seventeen when he was sold and now here he is at thirty. Imagine his patience growing? He had no idea what the future held, he could have gotten bitter and turned away from God. If he did, do you think he would have seen what was about to take place? Picture it, a dungeon. In those days, being in prison did not mean three squares, a college education, and basketball. It meant no food, or maybe bread and water, living with the rats and being chained to the floor.

Lesson #15 Can We Still Believe God's Promises After All These Years?

Could Joseph still believe? Can we still believe? Can you still believe? There seemed to be no hope no future? He had scars on his feet from the shackles, lots of scars on his back. A few years before he was thrown into prison, he was Potiphar's right-hand man and now, he hated him for something he didn't do. "When Joseph was tried and tested time and again, and could release all of his feelings to God to be able to trust Him, that is when He restored his prophetic gift which later was the key to his deliverance and his promotion to governor all of Egypt. He became the second in command which saved his entire family and the many generations thereafter."

I love the last part of this story. Joseph was tried and tested year after year until he could finally release all to God, and this is when his breakthrough came. He had his battle scars, but he was changed! He was the man of God, He could use. God allowed Joseph to rule Egypt so that he saved his family.

He became a humble servant, and the one God used to preserve Egypt and Israel's future.

I know all about battle scars, both my husband and I have them. They may not be like Joseph's, but they are very real to me and my husband. Every time I look at my scar, I am reminded of the battle we have won!

I will never forget before surgery I stood in front of the mirror in our bedroom imagining myself with a huge scar across my stomach. Being a woman, I had to set my mind and prepare myself for that huge change. I had two C-sections and a partial hysterectomy, we all know how the doctor so carefully cuts the line to make sure it is a bikini cut. This one, however, was there to see. A few weeks after surgery I was looking at myself in the mirror; I had a scar from under my breastbone, down to my belly button and across the right side. The Lord impressed on my heart how he used me to give life to my whole family, just as he used Joseph to give life to his family. It was in different ways, with Joseph it was to prevent his family from starvation and with me, it was to give life through birth and organ donation. Yet, it was the same, to give of yourself.

These scars I have are the most beautiful scars anyone could ever have. When I look at my family and know what a blessing they are to me, I wouldn't think twice about having another scar. This revelation was so healing to me, it made me feel proud, not in a prideful way, but in a way that was secure in who I am, and in what the Lord had done. It is an honor to be used of God in such a tremendous way.

Life Application: I Have Grown

The Lord revealed to me today, March 2011, how I've grown. Three years ago I held my hands up to the Lord and said, "Why Me?" today I hold my hands up to the Lord and say, "Thank You Lord for choosing me." What a difference, what a revelation! Three years ago my heart was resentful, confused and full of fear. Today my heart is humbled, grateful and full of joy.

God has a plan and a purpose for everything we go through if we trust Him. Remember, the Lord is good, He is kind, He is compassionate, He is slow to anger and abounding in Love.

The will of God in your life will not always be what you are expecting. His plan for your life may not always be easy, or even what you think you deserve. Remember, it's not about you and what you want. It's about what God wants to accomplish through you? *"We are God's workmanship, created in Christ Jesus to do good works, which God prepared in advance for us to do"* *(Ephesians 2:10).*

Sometimes I found myself feeling resentful in my heart when many people told me God put Joe and me together because I was supposed to donate my liver to my husband. Do you know what? No matter how I felt, I had to come to terms that God had a larger plan and purpose for our marriage. Keep your eyes fixed on Him, look at the big picture and keep your thoughts focused on Him.

Joe and I have come to the point in our life, like I shared before, that whatever His will is, we want. We are confident and still expecting that because He loves us, He has a plan for our life, and promotion is on the way just as Joseph. I just told the Lord the other night, this is even two and a half years after surgery that there has to be a purpose for all we went through. Yes, it was to give my husband life, our daughters their father and me, my husband, yet there has to be something greater. For now, we will wait.

Debra Lynn Viteri

What Can Be Greater!

My Journal: Months have gone by and today is August 13th, 2011, what can be greater than being able to celebrate Bethany's sweet sixteen together with family and her friends. Jessica is now 13 and Bethany 16! What can be greater than being able to be a family? God blessed us with the desire of our heart and that was to celebrate their special birthdays together and to have a built-in swimming pool.

For eleven years, Joe and I talked about the idea of having a pool. We would go to pool stores and price them, clip out pictures from magazines and put them on the fridge, we would dream about where we would place it so that we would be able to enjoy it to the fullest. Finally, the miracle happened, in October of 2010; we were having a pool installed and here we were using this gorgeous pool for our daughter's birthday.

The celebration for Bethany's sweet sixteen was so beautiful. Our backyard was decorated in teal and white balloons with teal tablecloths. The day was gorgeous with so many flowers of all colors. Everyone had so much fun swimming, and seeing each other.

My brother-in-law Carlos and sister-in-law, Lynda, designed a beautiful CD of her life. We watched it together and after it was over, I wanted to thank everyone for coming but was so choked up I couldn't even speak. I had so much running through my mind of all the miracles of God.

Everything Joe and I have gone through since we have been married have always been by faith. When I think about how far we have come, my heart fills with so much gratitude. We have visions and dreams for our future and we believe they will be fulfilled. When I see the Lord's faithfulness, I know He is preparing us for something greater than we can ever imagine. For now, we will wait; wait patiently for the next move. When the Holy Spirit is ready, He will direct us.

CHAPTER 34

❧

Refining of Gold

I am convinced that these testing's we have faced have been allowed in our life. God does not cause trials to happen, He is a good and perfect God; however, these trials come because we live in an imperfect world. These trials will shape our character and prove to Him and us to see how committed we are to His ways. He will know if our character will endure. When we do endure and praise Him, no matter what the circumstance, only then can He trust us with power that comes from Him and Him alone.

I explained that we felt like we were thrown into the crucible of fiery fires, and I wanted to come out as pure gold. Gold can only be made pure by entering into the crucible where the refining process begins. Only when the temperatures reach a certain point of heat can silver and gold be refined; the heat we face in our lives can also bring change, to cleanse, purify and rid of all imperfections. This is a process we as Christians must undergo.

God wants us to be sanctified, and to be holy (Ephesians 3:17-20). He wants us to purify ourselves, even as He is pure. He is Jehovah-M'Kaddesh, Jehovah who sanctifies will give you the strength. For this is the will of God even your "sanctification" *a separation to God for holy character. "All who have this hope purify themselves, just as He is pure"(1 John 3:3).* He is coming back for a glorious church to be presented holy and spotless, a church that does not have spot or wrinkle. That we should be like Him when He appears (Jesus) and if we have this hope, we will purify ourselves and get ready as a bride prepares herself for her bridegroom. Christ is our bridegroom and we are His bride (Ephesians. 5:26-27).

When Joe and I were getting married a scripture that was read at our ceremony is from the book of Isaiah. *"I delight greatly in the Lord; my soul rejoices in my God. For he has clothed me with garments of salvation and arrayed me in a robe of righteousness, as a bridegroom adorns his head like a priest, and as a bride adorns herself with jewels (Isiah 61:10). Your God rejoices over you.*

How should I prepare myself? First of all, realize you cannot do it alone, realize your dependence is on the Lord and ask Him to help you. Take time to ask the Lord what you should do to sanctify yourself. Perhaps it's a bad attitude, and you know you should ask God for forgiveness. Maybe it's a wrong motive and it's only about you. Or maybe you need to ask for forgiveness to yourself, spouse, sibling or anyone you may be holding a grudge against.

God will cleanse your heart and give you a new beginning; by doing this you will be able to fight the good fight of faith. You are a precious child of the Most High King. Don't forget, in order to come into His Kingdom, you will be tried and tested.

Don't fear; the Lord is with you, and will be right by your side to help you come out a winner. You are a precious gem to the Lord and He only tries what is valuable.

"In you greatly rejoice, though now for a little while you may have had to suffer grief in all kinds of trials. These have come so that your faith- of greater worth than gold, which perishes even though refined by fire, may be proven genuine and may result in praise glory and honor when Jesus Christ is revealed" (1 Peter 1:6-7).

Life Application: Can you see it? Your faith is of greater worth than gold. Gold perishes even though refined by fire; don't let your faith perish.

Someone gave this story to me when I was part of a woman Bible group I found it so beautiful so I'd like to share the story of a scripture found in Malachi 3:3 "He will sit as a refiner and purifier of silver."

Silver Purified

"This verse puzzled some women in the Bible study and they wondered what this statement meant about the character and nature of God. One of the women offered to find out the process of refining silver and get back to the group at their next Bible Study. That week, the women called a silversmith and made an appointment to watch him at work. She didn't mention anything about the reason for her interest beyond her curiosity about the process of refining silver.

As she watched the silversmith, he held a piece of silver over the fire and let it heat up. He explained that in refining silver, one needed to hold the silver in the middle of the fire where the flames were hottest as to burn away all the impurities.

The women thought about God holding us in such a hot spot; then she thought again about the verse that says: "He sits as a refiner and purifier of silver." She asked the silversmith if it was true that he had to sit there in front of the fire the whole time the silver was being refined. The man answered that yes, he not only had to sit there holding the silver, but he had to keep his eyes on the silver the entire time it was in the fire. If the silver was left a moment too long in the flames, it would be destroyed. The woman was silent for a moment. Then she asked the silversmith, "How do you know when the silver is fully refined? He smiled at her and answered, "Oh, that's easy, when I see My image in it"

If today you are feeling the heat of the fire, remember that God has His eye on you and will keep watching you until he sees His image in you. –Unknown Author

Devotional: *"Through Fire and Through Water"* (Psalm 66:10, 12)

That which has great value must be tried and tested. When silver is refined, it is for your own good. All the tin and dross (that which is of lesser value) are taken out of it, resulting in the silver becoming sterling quality, and therefore much more precious. I have been doing the same with you. I have put you into the crucible of fiery trials from which there was no escaping and there I heated the fires seven-fold that you might become perfect before Me. Man does not see your flaws, but I do. Therefore, I am working in you to remove all that yet remains which would mar the perfect image of Christ in you. Not only have I put you in the fiery crucible, I have also put your ministry there. Your ministry and those who work with you are being tested in the fire, that all which is not of sterling quality shall be removed speedily. For time is short, and I will only have a holy and pure Bride serving Me in My temple. You have been passing through the most excruciating fires of your entire life. There have been fires without and fires within. Many times you have cried unto Me, "How long?" And it seemed as though the pain would never go away. But it will. Not even silver is tried forever. There comes that moment when it has been tried to perfection, and then it will surely be removed from the fire. Suddenly I will reach down and remove you from those fiery trials, and then they shall only be a memory.

The waters may seem to roll over your very soul, but fear not, you will not drown. You must come through the twofold trial of fire and water, that you might have the double portion, even the oil that will supply the light for your lamp in these dark days, for behold, I come quickly now! I am bringing you into a wealthy place in Me. You shall find your soul shall grow rich in My greatness in you. In that day you shall know that it has all come to you through your experiences of fire and water.

Question: How do you respond in the fire?

_____

Question: What areas in my life can I be more like Christ?

_____

_____

Ponder: You are valuable, a prized treasure of the Lord.

CHAPTER 35

My Hero

We will continue to believe for the mighty miracle for Joe's continued health and for this virus of hepatitis C which I call a demon, a beast to be destroyed. No matter what, we will always believe that God forgives all sins and heals all diseases. The Lord spoke to my heart again!

Devotional: *"All Iniquities- All Diseases." (Psalm 103:3, 4).*

In these evil days, when the wickedness of man is great and the imagination of the thoughts of his heart only evil continuously so that the earth is corrupt and filled with violence and all flesh has corrupted his way, I still will forgive anyone who comes to Me seeking for pardon. Whether it be a mother who has aborted her son, or a man who has betrayed the wife of his youth, or the religious man whose heart is filled with envy and jealousy over what I have done in his neighbor's life it makes no difference; I will forgive all who call upon Me with a sincere heart of repentance. Did Paul not say,

"Christ Jesus came into the world to save sinners, of whom I am chief" (1Timothy 1:15b)

In the same way, in these evil days, when the plagues have broken out and the pale horse is riding, whose rider's name is Death, who has the power to kill fourth part of the inhabitants of the earth (Revelation 6:8), I am able to intervene and heal anyone who is smitten by the plague, even in the last hour, if he will repent. There is no disease nor sickness nor beast *(virus)* so powerful that I cannot heal and deliver the sufferer from its power to kill if he will call upon Me with a sincere heart, and I know he will be strong enough to live a holy life after he is healed. There are some who repent of their sins on their "deathbed" whom I must take home, because, if I allow them to live, they would soon be influenced by their companions in sin to fall back into their old ways of sin and their end would be even worse. So do not ask Me to heal everyone. I know best-pray always "Thy will be done," especially as you come to these last days I have a plan for your life-a plan which is not completed yet. I want to add years to your life. Reach out and accept My healing power for your body, that you may be healed and enabled to fulfill My blueprint for your life.

Remember, if you have sinned, I will forgive you when you truly repent. If you are sick, no matter what sickness, I am able to heal you if you will truly live for Me. Do not despair. Receive your miracle of healing from Me today. It is yours. I died to redeem your life from destruction. *"Blessed is the man who perseveres under trial, because when he has stood the test, he will receive the crown of life that God has promised to those who love him" (James 1:12).*

God always encourages me from this devotional. Sometimes I feel as it was written just for me. Once again, the Lord is showing me to be patient through the book of James, he tells us to be patient! *"Be patient, then, brothers, until the Lord's coming" (James 5:7).* He reminds us how a farmer waits for the crops to yield its valuable harvest. He also reminds us how patient He is for autumn and spring rains. He tells us to be patient for the Lord is near. One of His last commands is to be patient and stand firm because the Lord's coming is near. Stand Firm! Don't give up! Being patient is not in our vocabulary, we want everything quick and easy. We have to keep in mind to the Lord *"a day is as a thousand years and a thousand years is as a day" (2 Peter 3:8).* God does not work on time; there is no time with Him. Be patient, ready and waiting to receive your miracle; God is a miracle working God. He is the only true God of eternity, and His Word will endure forever.

"We can rejoice, too, when we run into problems and trials for we know that they are good for us- they help us learn to be patient. And patience develops strength of character in us and helps us trust God more each time we use it until finally our hope and faith are strong and steady" (Romans 5:3,4 TLB).

I know we can never see how trials and problems can be good for us. We have such a small understanding. I would think that after I have gone through so much and have seen Gods hand move on behalf of my family that when problems arise I would be happy. I try to, yet my humanity sometimes still gets the best of me. I do cry and sometimes I feel weak, but after a little while, I gain my insight to the word and I get strength from the Lord to continue to hold on and believe.

The Scripture teaches us that patience develops strength of character and what? Helps us to trust God each day. That is the huge lesson we all are striving to learn to trust God with our life. When you realize He is your father and loves you dearly you will trust Him with everything and then our hope and faith will be strong.

"Trust in the Lord with all your heart and lean not on your own understanding in all your ways acknowledges Him and He will make your path straight" (Proverbs 3:5).

I Was Blown Away

My Journal: Today November 4th, 2011 is our third-year liversary. Praise You Jesus! Three years have gone so fast. We have so much to be thankful for, enjoying life to the fullest. Both my girls have never expressed their feelings to their dad or myself about what we have gone through. I know they are grateful, but they never conveyed their thoughts to us. I believe because it was too painful for them. Jessica, Joe and I were sitting at the dinner table discussing school and Bethany was in another room. I decided to get up and look through her schoolbooks to see if I could find a paper she had written. To my surprise, I found another one of her writings and began to cry. Jessica and Joe didn't know why I was so emotional but I couldn't help myself. **The title of her paper was**

"My Hero Is My Mother"

Three years ago my dad got very sick and needed a liver transplant. He was going to die if he did not have a donor within two months. My mom was afraid to be a living donor for him because she was afraid both of them would die in the operation. My dad was rapidly getting sicker and he only weighed 118 lbs. and had to learn to walk. My mom then decided to become a living donor and was checked to see if she reached all the requirements. The doctor said she was healthy enough to donate half of her liver, and they went on with the surgery. The surgeon said everything matched so perfectly it was like they were brother and sister. My mom is my hero because she donated half her liver to my dad and today they are both alive and we can be a happy healthy family!

By Bethany Viteri

I was so elated and grateful that my daughter saw me as her hero. After surgery, many people referred to me as a hero and I couldn't accept it, I felt odd when they said that to me. However, when I heard my daughter call me her hero and I read how she explained everything so beautifully, it touched my heart more than my words can express. My obedience and this experience has not only impacted and blessed Joe and myself but extended to our daughters and so many others.

A few months later, I was in Jessica's room helping her clean and found an essay written by her. I am so happy they have had to write essays in school. It has really helped them to express themselves. What's interesting to me is how they chose to write about our experience, this article was written back in 2009 almost one year after surgery. She had to answer a question,

What Was The Happiest Time In Your Life?

One happy time in my life was when my dad was better from his surgery. My dad had liver surgery. His liver was dying out and if he didn't get one he would soon die. My mom turned out to be his donor. A donor is someone who gives part of their liver to someone who needs it. It turns out my dad only needed a half of my mom's liver. It also turns out that the liver grows back rapidly and in the opposite direction. While my parents were in the hospital, I was staying at my friend's house and my sister was staying at her friend's house. It also wasn't easy to see my mom and dad going through that and we were in school! But, luckily our teachers were very understanding. That was one very happy time in my life. By Jessica Viteri

These two articles my daughters wrote are so precious, I thank God they have experienced the provision of the Lord and His faithfulness. Thank You Lord!

Debra Lynn Viteri

Affliction Draws Us

King David knew that affliction was good for him to go through. Yet, when we read the Psalms we can hear the pain he is going through. My husband pointed this Scripture out to me today, two months later, May 6th, Psalm 119:67-72 *"Before I was afflicted I went astray, but now I obey your word."* You are good and what you do is good. Teach me your decrees. Though the arrogant have smeared me with lies, I keep your precepts with all my heart. Their hearts are callous and unfeeling, but I delight in your law. *It was good for me to be afflicted so that I might learn your decrees.* The law from your mouth is more precious to me than thousands of pieces of silver and gold."

I can really understand what King David says, before we were afflicted was I digging in the Word? Was I learning to walk by faith and not by sight? Were we really trusting in God? Sort of, we were going about our day as normal. Who likes to be afflicted? Not me! Not my husband! When I think about it, this affliction has been good because it has taught us to trust in Jesus. This journey has been bittersweet. It has enabled us to dig deeper into the Word and put into practice what we believe. It had definitely challenged us to say, "Whose report shall we believe?" We shall believe the report of the Lord! This is my prayer, "Lord, help us to resist the enemy, cause us to be alert and help us to stand firm and steadfast. Thank You Lord for Your grace, even though we have to suffer, Thank You for making us strong and for restoring us."

Thank-You for helping us to say, "Affliction is good."

A. Grace: *"And the God of all <u>grace</u>, who <u>called you</u> to His eternal glory in Christ, after you have <u>suffered</u> a little while, <u>will himself restore you and make you strong, firm and steadfast.</u> To him be the power forever and ever. Amen!"(1 Peter 5:10).*

B. *Strong and Firm:* *See it? You will become strong, firm and steadfast.*

My husband was so joyful today, as he read to me how we all should know the will of God.

"Be joyful always, pray continually, give thanks in all circumstances for this is God's will for you in Christ Jesus" (1 Thessalonians 5:16).

If only we could all be like that! Do you want to be in the will of God? Then be joyful, pray, and give thanks when all is going well! No! Give thanks in all circumstances and pray continually. My prayer life is not one of constantly kneeling and bowing before the Lord although that does have its proper time, to pray continually mean to always have a prayerful heart. I am constantly talking to the Lord throughout the day. As you practice these principles, you will be joyful because prayer can unlock the treasure chest of God's wisdom. God does promise to answer.

The Bible declares *"Call upon me and I will show you great and mighty things" (Jerimiah 33:3).*

God is good and so loving to all; even through life's blessing, trials, struggles, and victories. I have to remind myself of that at times, as I think about everything we have overcome and all that God has given us we stand in awe by His kindness. Writing about all our miracles makes me mindful of that fact.

CHAPTER 36

※

A New Beginning!

My Journal: Today is January 1, 2012. A New Year! We believe and trust the Lord for good things. Last night, we all went to the candlelight service at our church. We love bringing in the New Year in the presence of the Lord. Pastor Gary Zarlengo, who is extremely dedicated and committed to shepherding God's people, brought us a word from the Lord for the New Year. The word was to "Hold on" yes Lord, we will hold on and not look back, we will press on to the high calling in You. We will hold on and not give up! It was a time of rededication to the hand of the Lord and in my heart, His Word was for us, as a family. To "hold on", He has mighty things in store for this New Year!

Today's reading from my devotional Day by Day has also confirmed the Word the Lord has given me throughout this book. The Scripture I quoted to you before was confirmed today. I will state it again, so it may go down deep in your mind and heart. *"But his delight is in the law of the Lord, and in his law doth, he meditate day and night. And he shall be like a tree planted by the rivers of water, that brings forth his fruit in his season; his leaf also shall not wither, and whatsoever he does shall prosper" (Psalm 1:1-6).*

Devotional: "Meditate On the Right Things"

"My beloved child, as you begin this year, be very careful to never let a single day go by without meditating on "the law of the Lord." Don't only do it now and then, but heed the words that I spoke through My servant in this Psalm and meditate upon these things day and night. You will be saved many heartaches and sins if you will meditate upon that which is lovely and pure. Keep your mind on Me and on that will bless you and lift you. If you will observe this law of righteousness, even delighting and meditating on Me and My word, you will put your roots down deep into the source of truth and strength and health for your body, your soul, and your spirit. You will flourish in every way. Your life will be fruitful, and you shall become beautiful.

Life Key: There are so many truths to practice and take to heart. One major area we have to change is our thinking. I've said it before and I will say it again. When we are cast down it is because we have allowed our minds to get entangled with the things of this world. We have decided what dictates our emotions. I have gotten to this place several times, feeling burdened with life's cares. When I decide to change my thinking toward the Lord, my whole countenance changes and then I can walk in victory and peace. Let us count our blessings and name them one by one you will be amazed of the faith you will receive. Do not allow your mind to think about the negative. Rather think on that which is good and pleasant. Begin this year by counting up the blessings of the past year. The Lord wants you to know, He wants to bless you and prosper you. In this scripture above lies the key to all blessings. It holds the key to a long life, as you meditate and rejoice in God,

This passage is also the key to prosperity, if you meditate on God, whatsoever you do shall prosper. He wants to bless you in all that you do. Put God first in your heart and you shall be blessed in all ways. Finally, this passage is the key to happiness, for as you meditate on heavenly things your heart will be filled with joy, praise, and gratitude. Take hold, and take to heart this devotion and you will live, prosper and increase. You will live full and satisfied and you will live in the joy of the Lord."

My Journal: Today is July 31, six months has gone by since I have written. My husband went for his blood work a few days ago and now anxious thoughts are beginning to override his faith. Anticipation mixed with faith and a little fear are trying to waver him from continuing to believe. It's normal to go through periods of feeling anxiety and fear especially when this journey has had so many ups and downs. When we begin to think of what could take place it begins to overwhelm us.

The anxiety he is feeling is because this particular day he was talking to individuals who were not speaking faith to him but rather a concern. They wanted him to start the treatment, rightly so, I understand where they are coming from. We are deciding if we should take it now, however, as I explained before, this medication would be a trial, there are no guarantees that it would work and possibly even cause liver rejection. The doctors have also not given us a clearance to begin.

That afternoon, my husband and I again cried out to the Lord. He poured his heart out and asked the Lord in desperation "Lord, why aren't You healing me?" It has been a long, hard road. Year after year, and time after time we believe and yet it still seems to remain. After he poured his heart out to the Lord he repented in reverence because he knows God can complete the work in him. A peace filled our hearts and we were able to complete the day in trust and resting in Him in His presence. That morning I had read a portion of the Bible and was able to encourage him to keep the faith. We were encouraged again by the story of Abraham.

Abraham and his wife Sarah only were able to see the miracle of the promise when their bodies were as good as dead. "For many years, his faith stood the test of waiting while God repeatedly assured him of the promise." See it? Joe and I have stood the test of waiting, enduring, having patience for many years and God has repeatedly promised us His healing. We believe in the promises of the Lord God Almighty who is able to give us more than enough. He is all sufficient, all knowing and is able to revive the deadness of the body in order to show His great power.

I then said to him, do you want to be an Ishmael believing of the flesh? Or are you like Isaac believing by faith? There have been many days when he has to encourage me to keep the faith. Thank God we have always been able to encourage each other. Those that are of faith are sons of Abraham. God redeemed us so that the blessings given to Abraham might also come to the Gentiles through Christ Jesus so that by faith we might receive the promise of the Spirit. *"Therefore, those that are of faith are blessed with Abraham, the man of faith." Those who are of "faith" exercise faith, who is sons of Abraham, and we, therefore, are blessed with him, the man of faith. Who "against all hope believed and so became the father of many nations" (Romans 5:18).* All that are of faith are Abraham's children and heirs. If we hold the word with a firm grip, no one can snatch it away.

Lesson #16 Trust and Obey: The faith Abraham had was true, he **endured** many years, with his wife, the shame of not having any children, and **believed,** even at 100 years old, that God would keep His promise. He **trusted** when all odds were going against him, He **obeyed** to the point of laying his son on the altar.

A. He Never Weakened In His Faith: although he did "face the fact" meaning he knew reality but continued to **hold on** to God, he was **fully persuaded** that

God had the power to do what He had promised"
(Romans 4:19-21). Abraham had to

B. **Wait Patiently:** until he saw the **promise fulfilled**. It wasn't until his flesh and his wife's flesh was as good as dead. He was 100 years old and his wife Sarah was 90. It seemed as though it was humanly impossible, it was too late according to the flesh. She even laughs with a mixture of doubt and hope. However, the El Shaddai, the Almighty, the one who is able to do "exceedingly abundantly above all that we think or ask" blesses them with their son, the heir of the promise, Isaac. Abraham is our forefather that we need to model after. His example of endurance, patience, and long-suffering has ministered to generations of people throughout the years, we can learn from him as we can learn from each other. These principles are what Joe and I are holding on to. If you look at the words I highlighted, you will understand what true faith is.

Faith

Faith is, **Trusting When All Odds Are Against You. Enduring, Believing, and Never Giving Up, Being Fully Persuaded and Through it all, Walking in Complete Obedience, Knowing God Has the Power to KEEP HIS PROMISES!**

The past few days have been a challenge to stay focused. It seems as though our eyes want to fix on other things instead of truth. We choose to walk in God's ways and wait for His intervention. We are expecting good things because God is Good! He is the author and finisher of our faith! We will not waver, we will stand, wait and hold on!

My Journal: Today is August 3rd, 2012 Joe went to his doctor to see him for his results and a physical. When the doctor read him his blood report, the doctor was extremely baffled and extremely surprised that his liver enzyme levels were NORMAL! The doctor said, "Joe, they read normal, what happened? My husband shared the Lord's healing power and gave Him glory. We are always quick to do that. The ALT level is 37 NORMAL! ALT range is 9-60. The ALT is an important marker of liver inflammation. Having normal liver enzymes and controlling inflammation is a crucial factor in changing the poor prognosis of hepatitis C. Inflammation causes fibrosis (scarring) which leads to cirrhosis. His AST level is 36 one point away from normal! The range is 10-35! AST exists in the liver, heart, and muscle. Praise the Living God! His levels haven't been normal in nine and a half years! TO GOD BE THE GLORY FOR THE GREAT THINGS HE HAS DONE!

Joe called me with the greatest news while I was working and I couldn't stop dancing and praising Jesus. We are "Living Proof" of the faithfulness of the Lord. We will continue to believe the report of the Lord! For the next three consecutive blood works within this year, the blood work has to read normal. If the tests show three normal readings, then medically we can believe the liver has rejuvenated itself and the inflammation is gone. Even before the blood work, this is what we believe and hold on to. We are continuing to believe for a total eradication of this virus.

I also need to explain, hepatitis is a difficult disease to understand and just because normal enzyme levels have been read, it doesn't mean the liver is healthy, it still could have inflammation and even cirrhosis. Even though we have been told this by the doctors, we are still extremely excited because they do use these enzyme levels to determine the severity of inflammation which will cause cirrhosis.

Hepatitis C is a demonic, foul virus which can hide even in the bone marrow while being treated. Nine and a half years ago years ago, when he had an undetectable viral load, it was never totally eradicated. After the medication is given the virus comes out and replicates even quicker with a vengeance. When Joe and I spoke about the virus, the verse that was quickened to my spirit was found in Hebrews. *"For the Word of God is living and active. Sharper than any double- edged sword, it penetrates even to diving soul and Spirit, joints and marrow; it judges the thoughts and attitude of the heart"* (Hebrews 4:12).

The joint is the thick, hard outer part of the bone. The marrow is the soft, inner, living part of the bone. God's Word is alive, and active it divides the soul and the spirit of a man. The Word breaks through the hardest part of man entering into the soft inner living part of man's heart. His Word then judges the attitude of the heart.

My Journal: We are so encouraged today, Thank-You Lord for helping us to always be careful to let our thoughts and attitudes magnify You. Thank You for helping us to go from faith to faith and from victory to victory. Nothing is too hard for Thee. You, oh Lord, are Jehovah-Nissi, my banner. Your victory is always won no matter what the odds.

Without this medication, medically it is impossible for the levels to read normal. You oh Lord, are faithful! You oh Lord are our all and all. You are El-Shaddai is there anything too hard for Thee? Thank You Lord; for keeping Your covenant with Your servants who walk before You with their whole heart. God, You blessed Noah, Abraham, Joseph, Daniel and so many others because they kept their heart fixed on You. Thank You Lord for helping Joe and I to keep our hearts fixed on You. We have our total dependence on You. We have been desperate for Your direct intervention. Thank You Lord; for proving Yourself.

Thank You Lord; for building Your character into our lives. You have trained us for war, You have taught us to fight, You have taught us the way of life which is perseverance, longsuffering, endurance patience, and steadfastness. Thank You Lord; for imparting your character into our lives. Thank You Lord that proven character has not disappointed us but has now renewed us and given us a hope. Your ways are true. Thank You for the maturity and stability You have engraved in our hearts which only came through suffering. You have made us stable and stronger. Thank You, Lord we did not give in to the whispers around us, but You placed a shield round and about us. Thank You for helping us to remain obedient.

We went through trials of water and fire but You have brought us out into a wealthy place. I see it, we were in a fight to give up, but we chose to continue to honor you. Just when we were able to release all to You, you have restored us so that You may now promote us to a new level of authority. The scars Joseph bore in prison always reminded him of his battle he won and the favor of the Lord. In the same way, our scars will always be a reminder of the battle we won and the favor of You, God Almighty; Jehovah Rapha our Lord God our healer.

MY POWERFUL MIRACLE

God never ceases to amaze me! Four months ago, Joe and I celebrated our fourth Liversary on November 4th, and on the 12th, I found out a huge part of our miracle to my story. My Mom has been looking for my father's Army papers and finally found them. Not only is my brother and mother's blood type "A" but my father is A too! All three immediate family members are "A" blood type; however, I am O positive just so I could donate to my husband.

This is an amazing physical miracle. Just think, all three immediate family members of mine are all "A" blood type and I'm O positive. That is a huge part of our miracle. If I were A, that would have prevented Joe from receiving his miracle. God designed me to have O blood because only He knew my future.

Miracles may not come as you want it to or how you think it will come. It will come as He plans and how He sees fit. Now I can say, even more than I could have a few months ago, it has truly been a miracle blessed by God. Our journey has truly been "Painful Tears of Joy." To God be the Glory for the Great things He has done!

Things to do: Hear the Word, Read the Word, Study the Word Memorize the Word and Meditate on the Word. The Word meaning BIBLE

Write the Bible verse that has meaning to you and that you will stand on in times of trials

_____

_____

_____

_____

CHAPTER 37

Pressing On

My Journal: Today March 12, 2013, we got our report back that . . . . His enzyme levels are rising! My story is one of our real life experiences and reality of trusting God through it all. You can see how our life is like a roller coaster, it goes up and down quite often, but I want to portray that although our journey of the hepatitis C virus continues to see-saw, our Spirit will remain stable and we will continue to walk by faith in victory and joy.

I really wanted to leave you with a healing but we will continue to persevere, have longsuffering, endurance, patience and believe for our promise. Maybe for a moment, we sway and feel our emotions drain, but then our heartfelt dedication to what we know and believe continues to hold us firm. The reason why this year is so critical is because it's been five years since the transplant, and I was told the liver may only last five years due to the virus infecting it again.

I have to admit, when we first heard the news, we were discouraged for a few hours. I was at work and needed to wipe my face from my tears. I left the room and went to our prayer room to be alone in the presence of God. When I walked into the prayer room I screamed and cried like a baby. I read the inscriptions on the wall that read," seek and you will find, knock and the door will be open, ask and you will receive."

As I sat in the room, all I heard beside myself was silence. I felt alone and desperate. I called on God, the one who said, "I am there" and said out loud, "God where are You?" We've been knocking, we've been seeking, we've been asking.

We've walked by faith and have spoken by faith. As the silence penetrated the room, I thought about what I heard someone once say about taking a test. When you are taking a test it is silent and the teacher does not speak to you because they want you to prove that you know the answer. God ultimately is our teacher and He will respond when He wants to, and how He wants to. We are the clay He is the potter. After a little while, I told the Lord I did love Him and I did trust Him. I composed myself and went back to work.

When I got home, Joe and I both talked about the truth of God. For a few moments, I was even feeling like maybe some of those people are right, healing is not for today. Some people hold firmly to the belief that God does not heal today, they say He only healed in what they refer to as "the day of miracles," a time when Jesus was on earth. When I said that, I felt as though something left me. Like a huge part of what I have believed for so long just became a lie. Then we both looked at each other and agreed we will not be moved by circumstances. We will remain steady and fixed!

Healing Is For Today and Is The Children's Bread (Inheritance)

Thousands of generations can account for His healing touch. We will continue to pray for God's healing touch for our family and others. As you wait for your miracle or answer from God, Seek His presence, He will give you the faith you need. Always remain in Him even when you don't receive your healing, have patience and be a part of church where you can receive faith. Don't stop going, this is when you need it the most. *Faith comes by hearing and hearing comes by the word of God* (Romans 10:19).

Get Prayer From The Elders Of Your Church

Have the elders anoint you with oil (James 5:14-16). Remember God's delays are not always denials. Sometimes God has a larger purpose, results in His greater glory. Keep your heart pure with God and friends and praise Him anyhow! He deserves our praises!

How Do We Get Answered Prayer?

Life Application: God gives us requirements for answers to our prayer. **You must abide with Him.** That means to remain in His perfect will at ALL cost.

Romans 12:1,2 His words are to abide in you, they are to become a part of your life. You are to be filled with and guided by His words. If you do these things your prayers will be answered. I must warn you though

A. Immediate: Sometimes the answer is immediate. Ex: When Jesus went to Peter's house and touched his mother in law's hand. Instantly the fever left her and she got up and began to serve them. Matthew 8:14.

I remember an experience in my own life when I hurt my back really bad. I was on the floor doing something and when I tried to get up I couldn't move I was in really bad pain. I cried out to God to heal me and all of a sudden instantly, I was able to stand up and I was healed! I'll never forget it.

B. Delayed: Sometimes prayer is delayed. Yes, my book is filled with stories like this one. Be patient!

C. No: Sometimes the answer is No. When God answers you with a no, He always comforts you with His peace *"Do not be anxious for anything; but by prayer and petition, with thanksgiving, present your request to God. And the peace of God, which transcends will guard your hearts and your minds in Christ Jesus"* (Philippians 4:6, 7).

There have been so many times in my life I have prayed for something and the Lord did not answer my prayer so I took it as a "No" Now that I look back, I'm glad He didn't answer because it would have taken me off track from being in His will for my life. The answer is sometimes different from what you expect. I prayed for healing, instead, we had surgery. The Bible also says, *"Sometimes you ask you don't receive because you pray with the wrong motive"* (James 4:3). God answers ALL your prayers not according to your wishes, but according to His perfect will. Continue to persevere in faith and trust.

Life Key: Do not get angry if your prayer is not answered as you want it to; be willing to have it answered according to God's will. He knows best!

(Psalm 119:9-16). Most importantly, *"Keep your thoughts and eyes fixed on God and His ways the author and finisher of our faith..."* (Hebrews 12:2).

As I thought about my reaction to the news, I laughed at myself because I know I am far from being mature and complete, stable and unmovable. However, we are human and we all can act the same way. We all can get upset and restless in the process of our development and growth, but after we convey our feeling let's keep on pressing toward our goal. God is with you, He promised never to leave you. Every day is a new day to have strength, to become better, stronger and wiser. Perseverance is the key.

Miracles

What does the Bible say about miracles? God's covenant of healing is revealed with the children of Israel when He said; I am the Lord that heals thee"

(*Exodus 15:26*). He said, "I am the God" in the present tense. He didn't say, "I was," "I will be," but "I am!" God is and always will be the healer. Whether a miracle occurs instantaneously, a process of time by prayer, by medical technology or by taking an individual home, God does heal yesterday, today, and forever.

If we don't give up, this is a promise from the Lord if we continue to persevere. *"Blessed is the man who perseveres under trial, because when he has stood the test, he will receive the crown of life that God has promised to those who love him"*

As we go through our trials and testing we have to choose in our sufferings that we will do what God has asked us to do; to stand and persevere. Our choice is to run until we cross the finish line. We are in a race to make it home. *"Don't you realize that in a race everyone runs, but only one person gets the prize? So run to win! All the athletes are disciplined in their training. They do it to win a prize that will fade away, but we do it for an eternal prize" (1 Corinthians 9:24-25).* The prize that will last forever refers to the victory of eternal salvation. With this race, not only one will receive the prize, but we will all get it if we endure.

Life Application: We are all on our journey to live our life and in the process to become more like Him. We have particular circumstances to live; it is our choice to learn the virtues of Christ while going through them. Choose Christ in the midst of your suffering and He will help you to overcome.

In my own brokenness, His Word has come alive in my heart and Joe's heart. When you go through sickness and life's difficulties; God's Word will deepen and penetrate your heart if you allow it. We must learn not to grumble against God in the process, become a yielded broken vessel that He can put together and transform into His image. In return, He will pour His glory into you and use you for His Kingdom. He will give you the grace and the strength each day and a renewed vision. He will impart to you the courage to endure so that you can press on in life. Remember the quote I wrote in the beginning of this book?

"Faith Is A Faith That Will Stand No Matter What God Will or Will Not Do."

Our love for Him will remain stable and unmovable. We are that tree that has its roots deep in the Word of God that cannot be moved. You can make the same proclamation while going through your trials too.

"Praise be to the God and Father of our Lord Jesus Christ, the Father of compassion and the God of all comfort, who comforts us in all our trouble" (2 Corinthians 1:3-5).

Throughout my book, I have explained how we felt like we were placed in the chambers of fire and death, however, you have read my testimony to the Glory of God, how He was with us and never left our side. Just as He was with those three Hebrew boys in the fire, He has been with us. We will continue to proclaim the Good News of the gospel whether He rescues us or not.

No matter what the outcome, from a heart of gratitude and praise for God's gracious gift of salvation.

CHAPTER 38

Entering the Promise Land

I thought the last chapter was going to be the end of my book; however, God had another plan around the corner. If Joe and I gave up in the last chapter, we would have never entered the Promise Land.

Joe and I celebrated our 6 year Liversary today; it's now November 4th, 2014. This is a tremendous milestone in the transplant community. His enzyme levels have read normal for the last six months.

My Journal: Today, September 2014 we received a phone call from my surgeon Dr. Samstein, who told Joe there are new medications without interferon. He asked Joe to speak with his nurse practitioner to get him in for the trial. We are excited, this may be our answer. Finally, after almost twelve years, there is medicine to rid hepatitis C genotype 1a without interferon. It also could destroy the virus within a three-six month treatment. It seems like there is hope for us to be free from this virus. We were so grateful for the phone call.

For those who suffer from hepatitis C, the medical field has come out with remarkable therapy that can truly help

319

you before you need a transplant and even thereafter. Finally, this disease could be eradicated in millions of people's lives. "These new medications are known as "direct-acting antivirals." They act directly on the virus, rather than on his immune system like interferon. The medication destroys the virus by interfering with the ability to replicate and they are better tolerated and have been more effective against most genotypes." William Carey, M.D. Top Treatments Breakthroughs Magazine (Remedy Health Guides) p.11

My Journal: Today October 4, 2014, Joe went to the hospital for a checkup. He saw the nurse practitioner and talked to her about treatment. At first, she was reluctant about allowing him to be on the trial because he has a gene that is resistant to treatment, but after speaking with Joe, she agreed to call the doctor. Dr. Brown gave permission for Joe to be treated and we were also accepted by the insurance company the same day.

One of the criteria's before he begins treatment is, he has to have another biopsy. He really didn't want to have another biopsy; I'm sure it was because we had some fear of hearing the results. However, eventually he did have another biopsy and we were delighted to hear the liver looks good. It has NOT progressed further than stage two, slightly three in four years! Praise the Lord! We are so excited! His skin is also brand new, not one scar of any infection can be seen! Joe recently got the viral load count back and it decreased to 6800! Without medication, doctors continue to be astonished! We have peace this time and are excited about treatment to begin.

Praise God! Joe and I are continuing to anticipate what our future holds, we know it will be good and are looking forward to celebrating 21 years of marriage.

My Journal: Today, October 10th, 2014 Joe began treatment. I think it's kind of interesting, today is our 21 wedding anniversary. He went to New York-Presbyterian Hospital to begin treatment. The doctors want him to also take a combination of Ribavirin along with the other two medications. We really don't want him to take Ribavirin but they are concerned his virus won't respond due to the fact he has a resistant gene. This is all done by a trial, one of the medications is not FDA approved as of yet. They gave the hospital only a certain amount to try on some patients. They are not sure of the side effects, but we feel like this is the road we are to take. Sovaldi was approved in late 2013 and Daclatasvir has not been approved as of yet, but will be soon.

My Journal: After two days of taking the medication Joe is beginning to feel burned again, like a really bad sunburn and extremely itchy, muscle cramps and fatigue. Although the side effects are bad, they are not anything like the first time. We knew he shouldn't be on the Ribavirin but had to listen to the doctors' orders, however, when they saw him they immediately took him off and just kept him on the two.

The Promise Fulfilled!

His first blood work was taken on Tuesday, October 14, only four days into treatment and his virus is CLEARED! No signs of it anywhere! The doctors are so surprised; they never saw anyone respond so quickly. We are so excited and truly anticipating the days ahead.

My Journal: Joe is tired and healing from his reaction again, but doing well. We have had three labs done so far and the virus continues to be CLEARED! Praise the Lord! We have been waiting to hear this for so long! He has to stay on the medication for 24 weeks, but we are hoping the doctor will say he's finished in a shorter period of time. We are so excited because not only has the medication helped Joe, but now they know it will help thousands of other people with the same genotype and resistant gene. I love to hear my husband talking about one day being able to walk his daughters down the aisle and seeing his grandchildren. He has never talked about this before.

I know there are mighty plans for us down the road, and I know God will fulfill our dreams and visions we had so long ago. He is good!

Hold Onto Your Dreams and
Continue To Persevere
Until They Become A Reality.

Healing comes in many ways, like I told my daughters eleven and a half years ago supernaturally, medically or by taking you home where you truly will live in wholeness.

My Journal: Joe completed the treatment, he did have to complete 24 weeks. At times, his muscles hurt so bad it was hard for him to lift his arms up. He had some brain fog and sometimes tired, however, he was able to complete the treatment and he's still cleared of the virus. He has been taken off one rejection medication, Cellcept about one year ago and is truly doing so well. In another four weeks, we will have labs done again, this time with no medication and we believe the virus will continue to be eradicated.

God gave this scripture to Joe recently. He has never seen this one before.

"Oh Lord My God, I Cried Unto Thee
and Thou Hast Healed Me"
(Psalm 30:2).

I'm Healed!

Joe has been speaking by faith for years saying, "I am healed" now he can finally say, medically "I am healed."

My Journal: Today, April 24, 2015, we received the report of the blood lab that the virus is CLEARED! Without medication! Isn't it interesting that again the month is April? April 2003 he was diagnosed with hepatitis, April 2010 he was diagnosed the second time back in stage 2/3 and now, he is healed in April 2015.

The Lord showed me today, how I did receive a supernatural miracle. This whole journey has been extraordinarily super and extremely natural by every meaning of the word. God sure does have a sense of humor.

Seven Is God's Perfect Number,
2008 Transplant-2015 Healed = 7
Praise The Lord!

This is my recent family picture, God is good! Bethany is now 20 and in her third year attending Liberty University, Jessica is seventeen, a senior in High school, planning to attend Liberty next year. Joe and I look forward to many years of completing the work of the Lord!

Family Picture

I want to leave you with this scripture
that truly sums up my book

**"The crucible for silver and the furnace
for gold, but the Lord tests the heart"
(Proverbs 17:3).**

"Painful Tears of Joy" has been written through just that, deep pain and tears which eventually became joy and will continue to be for the glory of God. We are called to be a living testament, a living sacrifice for Him. **"I urge you brothers, in view of God's mercy, to offer your bodies as a living sacrifice, holy and pleasing to God-this is your spiritual act of worship. Do not be conformed any longer to the patterns of this world, but be transformed by the renewing of your mind. Then you will be able to test and approve what GOD'S WILL IS, HIS GOOD, PLEASING and PERFECT WILL"** (Romans 12:1).

Closing Thoughts

I love you all and pray God will give you the endurance to persevere and to come out as refined gold ready for the Master's use.

Encouraging Words

I hope and pray you have been encouraged and inspired as you have read about God's provision in my life. Know the same miracles God has shown me He can also do for you. They may come in different ways, but know, He loves you as His own. He has called you by name. He knows how you were created for He created you in His own image. He has a plan and purpose for your life from the moment you were born.

As you are walking life's road of triumphs and tragedies, victories and defeats, always remember to choose life. By choosing life, He will fill you with His grace, victory and peace even when it seems impossible. You will be able to walk in new heights and a new direction for your life. He doesn't want you to stay the same broken and full of pain, He wants you to grow in life's challenges and in the knowledge of the Lord. This will enable you to receive the joy of the Lord. It will be possible to have peace in your heart knowing He will ultimately guide your every step, fill you with strength and direct your life where it seemed impossible.

My Prayer For You

Heavenly Father, I come to You on behalf of my dear readers, who are suffering in this world. Give strength to the weak and comfort to the broken hearted. Restore their love for You, and give them a deeper commitment to serve You no matter what life may bring. Guide and fill them with Your perfect peace and wisdom. I ask You to make their path clear and give them understanding to overcome to be victorious. Thank You Lord that You hear their cry and that You promise "weeping may last for a night but joy comes in the morning."

Thank You for your blood that heals and for Your power to overcome. Help my dear readers to lay their dreams and desires at the foot of Your cross. Thank You that You already paid the price so we may walk in victory. Thank You Lord that it is not by might, nor by power, but by Your Holy Spirit and we can rest assure You have us covered and You are in control.

Give us the ability to see with the Spirit and not with the flesh, help those in need today to give their desires and dreams to You, so that You can fulfill the blueprint for their life. Cause our eyes to be fixed on You and our thoughts to be dedicated to think of things that are from above. Thank You Lord for Your healing power that reaches to the ends of the earth; fill my readers with strength to walk in peace, joy and victory. In Jesus mighty Name and in the power of the Holy Spirit, Amen!

If you have read this book and you do not know if you have eternal life and would want the assurance of knowing where you will go in this next life; before you pray with me I would like to explain a little more in detail about salvation.

God is a Holy God and cannot look upon sin. He had to send a redeemer to be a mediator between man and God. He sent Jesus Christ through his Jewish servant Mary. I love her heart she was willing to be used of God even if it brought ridicule from family and friends. **She believed with her whole heart that what God said would be accomplished.**

This is another huge lesson we can learn from Mary. This child, Mary, and Joseph had grew in stature and wisdom. He came to earth so that, by Him, we could be made righteous. Another name for God is Jehovah-Tsidkenu, our righteousness. We could never be made righteous on the basis of our own works, God sent His son to take our punishment. His righteousness is bestowed upon us as a free gift through faith. We are seen as righteous because of the Blood of Christ, we are cleansed with His blood and made righteous, right standing with God. He had to pour out His blood for you and me.

Mary gave birth to Jesus who was born for one purpose and that was to be obedient even unto death on the cross. Can you imagine Mary's obedient heart? Not only was she ridiculed from people, but the fact she raised Jesus as her on "son" and then had to watch him die on the cross. As his mother, she was always there for him, but at that moment, she could not prevent Him from being put to death.

He took humanities sins upon His shoulders and therefore we can stand before the Father totally spotless. It has nothing to do with what you or I can do, but it's all because of what Jesus did for us on the cross. People may say, "I'm a good person, or, I lived a good life, I never hurt anyone." That's all good; we should be a good person. However, works are not a source of our justification. It is strictly by faith in what the Messiah, Christ, did on the cross. Justification comes as a result of believing in Him. Justification is a promise to all who believe. It deals with the new position of the restored believer. To all who respond by faith will receive the benefits of God's grace, which is standing in His presence just as if you had never sinned, knowing God has forgiven you of your past sins and that He remembers them no more. This allows us to come boldly before the throne of God. It becomes a throne of grace rather than the throne of judgment.

Through Christ's blood, we can stand before Him free and clean. Justification does not only have to do with putting away our guilt, but also a new place and standing. It is an immediate gift. It comes through faith the moment you believe and receive Him. Since God has justified us by faith and not by works, we can have peace with God both in our heart and conscience. Why?

If our salvation was based on works, we fall so short many times. *"For since he himself has now been through suffering and temptation, he knows what it is like when we suffer and are tempted, and he is wonderfully able to help us"* (Hebrews 2:18).

This explanation is simple and now you can say this simple prayer and be assured of your new birth.

Jesus, I know I am a sinner and I am in need of a Savior. Please forgive me of my sins and dwell in my heart. Thank You for dying on the cross and for taking my penalty for me. Thank You for giving Yourself so that I may be free.

I declare today that I am born again and that I will serve You with all that is within me. I am a child of God set free to serve You.

Thank You, Jesus Amen!

A Prayer From The Author: In the Precious Name of Jesus I declare today, you will no longer listen to lies and negative reports. You are a child of God! Be filled with peace and joy in the Holy Spirit, and by His stripes, you are healed. In Jesus mighty Name, Amen!

(Read this prayer again and place the word I or your name where you see the word they).
It will become personal to you

Bibliography

Questions and Answers for patients and families about
MELD and PELD. Richmond, VA: United Network for
Organ Donation (UNOS used by permission

Scripture is taken from the Living Bible copyright 1971
by Tyndale House Foundation. Used by permission of
Tyndale House Publishers, Inc., Carol Stream Illinois
60188 All rights reserved

Scripture is taken from the HOLY BIBLE, NEW
INTERNATIONAL VERSION. Copyright 1973, 1978,
1984 International Bible Society. Used by permission
of Zondervan Publishing House.

Shaw, Gwen R. Day by Day, A Daily Praise Offering: Jasper,
ARK, End-Time Handmaidens, Inc. Engeltal Press
Copyright 1987. used by permission

Zhang, Qingcai. Healing Hepatitis C: With Modern Chinese
Medicine. New York: Sino-Med Institute, 2000. Print.
Used by permission

Contact Information

American Liver Foundation 30 Broadway #2700 New York, NY 10006 (212) 668-1000 www.liverfoundation.org

Center for Liver Disease and Transplantation.
New York-Presbyterian Hospital/Columbia University Medical Center,
Living Donor Liver Transplantation.
622 West 168th Street New York, NY 1002-3784;
(212-342-5149)

Chinese Herbs
Qingcai, Zhang, M.D.
20 E46 Street, suite 1402
New York, NY 10017
212-573-9584

United Network for Organ Sharing:

1-804-782-4800, www.unos.org (Organ Sharing)

To contact the author for speaking engagements, prayer and counsel please visit our website at:
www.DebraViteriauthor.com

To God be the Glory!   Joe & Debbie Viteri

Biography

Debra Viteri is a graduate of Christ For The Nations Bible Institute and Empire State University and is currently the Director of Smithtown Christian School Early Learning Center.

Through her writings, she wants to demonstrate how fear, anxiety, and hopelessness can be turned to peace, joy and hope in the midst of your confusion and despair.

Her desire is for you to be victorious over life's tragic circumstances. Debra presently resides in Hauppauge, Long Island with her husband and two daughters.

Printed in the United States
By Bookmasters